Table of Contents
at-a-glance

Turn to Page 1 of each chapter for a
DETAILED TABLE OF CONTENTS

D0917857

PREFACE

In this new millennium, critical care practitioners (respiratory therapists, nurses, physicians, etc.) are faced with astounding advances in knowledge and technology of critical care. Expanding rules, increased responsibilities, and the multi-disciplinary team approach demand a proper understanding of the principles and practice of hemodynamic monitoring.

The measurement, interpretation, and integration of hemodynamic parameters have become a common and essential ingredient of appropriate and effective patient evaluation and critical care management.

This book is a compilation and summarization of current principles and practices. It is not designed to be comprehensive or explanatory, but rather quick reference in nature.

It is essential, therefore, that the user have a working knowledge of cardiopulmonary anatomy, physiology, assessment, pathophysiology, and clinical management, as well as some specialized training in critical care.

It must be remembered that hemodynamic monitoring is an adjunct tool in assessing and evaluating the patient's pathophysiological status. Interpretation of hemodynamic parameters must, therefore, be evaluated with caution and in light of individual variations, coexisting pathological conditions, and possible monitoring errors.

Critical care diagnosis and management should never be based on hemodynamic parameters alone, but rather on the total patient picture.

It is hoped that this bedside reference manual will heighten the comprehension and competence of all critical care providers, enhance application of hemodynamic monitoring, and add greater precision to the diagnosis and therapeutic management of patients.

Dana Oakes

1 Overview of Hemodynamic Parameters

Purpose of Hemodynamic Monitoring:
To assess a patient's cardiopulmonary system

ABBREVIATIONS

Symbols and Acronyms*

$A-aDO_2$ ....alveolar-arterial oxygen tension difference
ABG.............arterial blood gas
A-line ....arterial catheter
AoD.............aortic diastolic pressure
AoM............mean aortic pressure
AoS ....aortic systolic pressure
ASD ....atrial septal defect
a-v...............arterio-venous
$a-vDO_2$ ....arterio-venous oxygen tension difference
$a-\bar{v}DO_2$ ....arterio-mixed venous oxygen tension difference

BP ....blood pressure, arterial
$\overline{BP}$ ....mean arterial blood pressure
BP dia.........arterial diastolic blood pressure
BP mean .....(see $\overline{BP}$)
BP sys.........arterial systolic blood pressure
BSA ....body surface area

CAD.............coronary artery disease
CAPP ....(see CPP)
CaO_2............arterial oxygen content
$Ca-vO_2$.........arterio-venous oxygen content difference
$Ca-\bar{v}O_2$.........arterio-mixed venous oxygen content difference
CBF ....coronary blood flow
CHF ....congestive heart failure
CI ....cardiac index
CO...............cardiac output
CO_2..............carbon dioxide
COP............colloid osmotic pressure
COPD ....chronic obstructive pulmonary disease
CPAP ....continuous positive airway pressure
CPP ....coronary perfusion pressure
CPR ....cardiopulmonary resuscitation
CV ....cardiovascular
CvO_2............venous oxygen content

* Most commonly used throughout the medical literature.

C$\overline{v}$O$_2$............mixed venous oxygen content
CVP.............central venous pressure
CXR.............chest x-ray

DO$_2$.............oxygen delivery (O$_2$ transport)
DOE.............dypnea on exertion
DPG (2,3)....2,3 diphosphoglycerate

E.................expiration
EDP.............end diastolic pressure (see LVEDP or RVEDP)
EDV.............end diastolic volume (see LVEDV or RVEDV)
EF................ejection fraction
EKG (ECG) ...electrocardiogram
ESP.............end systolic pressure
ESV.............end systolic volume
ET...............endotracheal tube

FIO$_2$ ....fraction of inspired oxygen
FO$_2$Hb ....fractional oxyhemoglobin
FP...............filling pressure (see LVFP or RVFP)

HD..............heart disease
Hgb ....hemoglobin
HR...............heart rate

I...................inspiration
IABP............intra-aortic balloon pump
IMV............intermittent mandatory ventilation
IVC ....inferior vena cava

JVD.............jugular vein distension

LA................left atrium
LAP..............left atrial pressure (usually mean)
LH ....left heart
LHF..............left heart failure
LOC ....level of consciousness
L-R..............left to right (shunt)
LV ....left ventricle
$\overline{LV}$P ....mean left ventricular pressure
LVEDP..........left ventricular end diastolic pressure

LVEDV ....left ventricular end diastolic volume
LVF ....left ventricular failure
LVSP ....left ventricular systolic pressure
LVSV ....left ventricular systolic volume
LVSW...........left ventricular stroke work
LVSWI..........left ventricular stroke work index

MAP............mean arterial pressure (see also BP)
MȮ$_2$ ....myocardial oxygen delivery
MI ....myocardial infarction
MPAP ....mean pulmonary artery pressure (see PAMP)
MV̇O$_2$ ....myocardial oxygen consumption

O$_2$................oxygen
O$_2$CT............oxygen content
O$_2$ER............oxygen extraction ratio
O$_2$SAT ....oxygen saturation
OUC ....oxygen utilization coefficient (see O$_2$ER)

P.................pressure
P50 ....pressure at which hemoglobin is 50% saturated
Pa...............arterial pressure
PA ....alveolar pressure
PA...............pulmonary artery
PaCO$_2$..........arterial carbon dioxide tension (pressure)
PADP ....pulmonary artery diastolic pressure
PAEDP ....pulmonary artery end-diastolic pressure (see PADP)
PAMP ....pulmonary artery mean pressure
PAOP ....pulmonary artery occlusion pressure (see PAWP)
PaO$_2$............arterial oxygen tension (pressure)
PAO$_2$............alveolar oxygen tension (pressure)
PAP ....pulmonary artery pressures
P̄AP ....pulmonary artery mean pressure (see PAMP)
PAP dia........pulmonary artery diastolic pressure (see PADP)
PAP sys........pulmonary artery systolic pressure (see PASP)
PASP............pulmonary artery systolic pressure
PAWP ....pulmonary artery wedge pressure
PB ....barometric pressure
PCHP ....pulmonary capillary hydrostatic pressure
PCWP..........pulmonary capillary wedge pressure (see PAWP)
PDA.............patent ductus arteriosus

PEEP............positive end-expiratory pressure
PFP..............pulmonary filling pressure (see RVEDP)
pH................hydrogen ion concentration
pHa ....hydrogen ion concentration of arterial blood
pHv ....hydrogen ion concentration of venous blood
PH_2O ....water vapor pressure
P_{IC}..............intracardiac pressure
P_{IO_2}.............inspired oxygen tension (pressure)
P_{IP}...............intrapleural pressure
PIP ....peak inspiratory pressure
P_{IT}...............intrathoracic pressure
P_{IV}..............intravascular pressure
PMI ....point of maximal impulse
PND............paroxysmal nocturnal dyspnea
PP ....pulse pressure
PPV ....positive pressure ventilation
PSVT...........paroxysmal supraventricular tachycardia
P_{TcCO_2} ....trancutaneous carbon dioxide tension (pressure)
P_{TcO_2} ....trancutaneous oxygen tension (pressure)
P_{TM}............transmural pressure
Pv................venous pressure
$P\bar{v}$................mixed venous pressure
PV ....pulmonary veins
$PvCO_2$..........venous carbon dioxide tension (pressure)
$P\bar{v}CO_2$..........mixed venous carbon dioxide tension (pressure)
PvO_2...........venous oxygen tension (pressure)
$P\bar{v}O_2$...........mixed venous oxygen tension (pressure)
PVP ....mean pulmonary venous pressure (same as PAWP)
PVR ....pulmonary vascular resistance
PVRI ....pulmonary vascular resistance index

RA ....right atrium
RAP ....right atrial pressure (usually mean) (see $\overline{RAP}$)
$\overline{RAP}$ ....mean right atrial pressure
RBBB..........right bundle branch block
RH ....right heart
RHF ....right heart failure
R-L...............right to left (shunt)
RPP ....rate pressure product
RR ....respiratory rate

RV ....right ventricle
RVEDP ....right ventricular end-diastolic pressure
RVEDV.........right ventricular end-diastolic volume
RVF ....right ventricular failure
RVP ....right ventricular pressure
$\overline{RVP}$ ....mean right ventricular pressure
RVSP ....right ventricular systolic pressure
RVSV ....right ventricular systolic volume
RVSW ....right ventricular stroke work
RVSWI.........right ventricular stroke work index

SaO_2 ....arterial oxygen saturation
SFP..............systemic filling pressure (see LVEDP)
SOB.............shortness of breath
SpO_2 ....saturation of oxygen via pulse method
SV................stroke volume
SVC ....superior vena cava
SVI...............stroke volume index
SvO_2 ....venous oxygen saturation
$S\overline{v}O_2$ ....mixed venous oxygen saturation
SVR ....systemic vascular resistance
SW ....stroke work
SWI ....stroke work index

TMG............transmyocardial pressure gradient

UO ....urinary output

$\dot{V}A$ ....minute alveolar ventilation
$\dot{V}E$................minute ventilation
VEDP..........ventricular end diastolic pressure (see LVEDP or RVEDP)
VEDV...........ventricular end diastolic volume (see LVEDV or RVEDV)
$\dot{V}O_2$ ....oxygen consumption (demand)
VS................vital signs
VSD ....ventricular septal defect
VT ....tidal volume

WOB ....work of breathing

HEMODYNAMIC MONITORING PARAMETERS
(Terms, Abbreviations, Symbols, Values, Definitions, and Equations)

Parameter	Abbrev. or Symbol	Normal Values	Definition	Derivation Equation	Ref. Page #
Afterload (RV or LV)			Total force opposing ventricular ejection		2-34
Alveolar-arterial oxygen tension difference (gradient)	A-aDO$_2$	Room air: 10-25 mmHg (increases with age) 100% O$_2$: 35-45 mmHg (at sea level)	Partial pressure difference between oxygen in alveoli and oxygen in arterial blood	A-aDO$_2$ = PAO$_2$ - PaO$_2$ = PA-aO$_2$	2-7
Alveolar oxygen tension	PAO$_2$	Room air: 100 mmHg 100% O$_2$: 663 mmHg (at sea level)	Partial pressure of oxygen in alveoli	PAO$_2$ = [(P$_B$-PH$_2$O) FIO$_2$] - PaCO$_2$ · 1.25	2-7
Aortic diastolic pressure	AoD	60-80 mmHg	Diastolic BP measured at root of aorta		
Aortic mean pressure	AoM	70-90 mmHg	Mean BP measured at root of aorta		
Aortic systolic pressure	AoS	100-140 mmHg	Systolic BP measured at root of aorta		

Parameter	Abbrev or Symbol	Normal Values	Definition	Derivation Equation	Ref. Page #
Arterial carbon dioxide tension (pressure)	$PaCO_2$	35-45 mmHg (4.66-6.00 kPa)	Partial pressure of CO_2 dissolved in arterial blood		
Arterial hydrogen ion conc	pHa	7.40-(7.35-7.40)	Index of acidity or alkalinity of arterial blood	$pH = 1/log[H^+]$	
Arterial oxygen content	CaO_2	15-24 mL/dL	Total amount of oxygen in arterial blood (combined plus dissolved)	$CaO_2 = (SaO_2 \times Hgb \times 1.36) + (PaO_2 \times 0.0031)$	2-7
Arterial pressure	See blood pressure				
Arterial oxygen saturation	SaO_2 or O_2 sat	~ 95%-100%	Percent of hemoglobin in arterial blood saturated with oxygen		
Arterial oxygen tension (pressure)	PaO_2	80-100 mmHg (10.66-13.06 KPa)	Partial pressure of oxygen dissolved in arterial blood		
Arterio-(mixed) venous oxygen content difference	$Ca-\bar{v}O_2$	4.2-5.0 mL/dL	Difference between arterial and mixed venous oxygen contents (reflects O_2 consumption)	$Ca-\bar{v}O_2 = CaO_2 - C\bar{v}O_2$	2-7
Arterio-(mixed) venous oxygen tension difference	$a-\bar{v}DO_2$	≈ 60 mmHg	Difference between arterial and mixed venous oxygen tensions	$a-\bar{v}DO_2 = PaO_2 - P\bar{v}O_2$	
Atrial pressure	See left and/or right				

Parameter	Abbrev. or Symbol	Normal Values	Definition	Derivation Equation	Ref. Page #
Blood pressure — *Arterial* Systolic	BP sys	100-140 mmHg	Systemic arterial pressure during systole		2-20
Mean	$\overline{BP}$ or MAP	70-105 mmHg	Time-averaged arterial blood pressure	$$BP = \frac{BP\ sys + 2BP\ dia}{3}$$	
Diastolic	BP dia	60-80 mmHg	Arterial pressure during diastole		
Pulse pressure	PP	20-80 mmHg	Difference in pressure between systolic and diastolic	$PP = BP\ sys - BP\ dia$	
Body surface area	BSA		Area of body surface	Obtained from Dubois chart	
Carbon dioxide tension (pressure) — Arterial	$PaCO_2$		See arterial		
Mixed venous	$P\bar{v}CO_2$		See mixed		
Venous	$PvCO_2$		See venous		
Cardiac index	CI	2.5-4.4 L/min/m²	Cardiac output expressed per body surface area (more precise measure of pump efficiency than CO)	$CI = CO/BSA$	2-20

Parameter	Abbrev. or Symbol	Normal Values	Definition	Derivation Equation	Ref. Page #
Cardiac output	CO or Qt	4-8 L/min (at rest)	Amount of blood pumped by the heart per minute (indicator of pump efficiency and a determinant of tissue perfusion)	$CO = HR \times SV$	2-20
Central venous pressure	CVP	0-6 mmHg (0-8 cmH$_2$O)	Mean blood pressure in central veins and right atrium		6-1
Contractility			Force of ventricle contraction independent of effect of preload or afterload		2-36
Coronary blood flow	CBF	mL/min or per unit of myocardium	Perfusion of blood through the coronary arteries		2-17
Coronary (artery) perfusion pressure	CPP or CAPP	60-80 mmHg	Driving pressure of coronary blood flow	$CPP = MAP - PAWP$ or $= BP\ dia - PAWP$	2-18
Ejection fraction	EF	0.65 (65%) (50-75%)	Percentage of ventricular chamber emptying (amount of blood ejected per total volume) (Index of ventricular contractility)	$EF = SV/EDV \times 100$ or $= EDV - ESV/EDV \times 100$	2-26
End diastolic pressure	EDP	See LVEDP &/or RVEDP	Pressure in ventricle at end diastole		

Parameter	Abbrev. or Symbol	Normal Values	Definition	Derivation Equation	Ref. Page #
End diastolic volume	EDV	See LVEDV or RVEDV	Volume of blood in ventricle at end diastole	EDV = SV + ESV	
End systolic pressure	ESP	See LVESP and/or RVESP	Pressure in ventricle at end systole		
End systolic volume	ESV	See LVESV and/or RVESV	Volume of blood in ventricle at end systole	ESV = EDV − SV	
Fraction of inspired oxygen	FIO_2	0.21-1.00	Fraction of oxygen in inspired air		
Fractional oxyhemoglobin	FO_2Hb	Arterial: 0.94-0.97 (94-97%) Venous: 0.68-0.77 (68-77%)	Actual or measured oxyhemoglobin saturation (portion of total hemoglobin combined with oxygen)		
Heart rate	HR	60-100 beats/min	Number of heart beats/minute		2-25
Hydrogen ion concentration	See arterial and/or venous or mixed venous				
Left atrial pressure	LAP	4-12 mmHg	Mean blood pressure of left atrium		2-11

Parameter	Abbrev. or Symbol	Normal Values	Definition	Derivation Equation	Ref. Page #
Left ventricular end - diastolic pressure	LVEDP	4-12 mmHg	Pressure in left ventricle at end diastole (reflects LV preload)		2-29
Left ventricular end - diastolic volume	LVEDV	Can't measure clinically	Volume of blood in left ventricle at end diastole		2-29
Left ventricular end - systolic pressure	LVESP	100-140 mmHg	Pressure in left ventricle at end systole		2-11
Left ventricular end - systolic volume	LVESV	Can't measure clinically	Volume of blood in left ventricle at end systole		
Left ventricular function curve			Plot reflecting cardiac output to LV preload		2-31 2-36
Left ventricular stroke work	LVSW	60-80 gm/m/beat	Work performed by LV (measure of LV performance)	$LVSW = SV \times (\overline{BP} - PAWP) \times 0.0136$	2-26
Left ventricular stroke work index	LVSWI	40-75 gm/m/beat/m²	Work performed by LV per body surface area (indicator of LV contractility)	$LVSWI = LVSW / BSA = SVI \times (\overline{BP} - PAWP) \times 0.0136$	2-26 2-36
Mean arterial pressure	$\overline{BP}$ or MAP	See blood pressure, mean			

Parameters

Parameter	Abbrev. or Symbol	Normal Values	Definition	Derivation Equation	Ref. Page #
Mean pulmonary artery pressure	PAMP	See pulmonary artery pressure, mean			
Mixed venous carbon dioxide tension (pressure)	$P\bar{v}CO_2$	46 mmHg (41-51 mmHg)	Partial pressure of carbon dioxide in mixed venous blood		
Mixed venous hydrogen ion concentration	$pH\bar{v}$	7.36 (7.31-7.41)	Index of acidity or alkalinity of mixed venous blood	$pH = 1/\log[H^+]$	
Mixed venous oxygen content	$C\bar{v}O_2$	12-15 mL/dL	Total amount of oxygen in mixed venous blood (combined plus dissolved)	$(S\bar{v}O_2 \times Hgb \times 1.36) + (P\bar{v}O_2 \times 0.0031)$	2-7
Mixed venous oxygen saturation	$S\bar{v}O_2$	75% (68-77%)	Percent of hemoglobin in mixed venous blood saturated with oxygen	$S\bar{v}O_2 = SaO_2 - \dfrac{VO_2}{DO_2}$	3-8
Mixed venous oxygen tension	$P\bar{v}O_2$	35-42 mmHg (4.66-5.60 KPa)	Tension exerted by dissolved oxygen in mixed venous (PA) blood		3-10
Myocardial oxygen consumption (demand)	$M\dot{v}O_2$	ml/min/100 gm of myocardium	Amount of O_2 consumed (utilized) by the heart per minute		2-18
Myocardial oxygen delivery (supply)	$M\dot{D}O_2$		Amount of O_2 delivered to heart by coronary vessels		2-17

Parameters

Parameter	Abbrev. or Symbol	Normal Values	Definition	Derivation Equation	Ref. Page #
Oxygen consumption (demand)	$\dot{V}O_2$	200-250 mL/min	Amount of O_2 consumed (utilized) by the body per unit time (minute)	$\dot{V}O_2 = CO \times Ca - \bar{v}O_2 \times 10$	2-7
Oxygen consumption index	$\dot{V}O_2I$	110-165 mL/min/m²	Oxygen consumption per body size	$\dot{V}O_2 \cdot CI \times Ca - \bar{v}O_2 \times 10$	
Oxygen content	O_2CT	See arterial and/or mixed venous oxygen content and arterio-venous O_2 content difference			
Oxygen delivery (supply or transport)	$\dot{D}O_2$	750-1000 mL/min	Quantity of O_2 pumped by the heart to body tissue per unit time (minute)	$\dot{D}O_2 = CO \times CaO_2 \times 10$	2-7
Oxygen delivery index	$\dot{D}O_2I$	500-600 mL/min/m²	Oxygen delivery per body size	$\dot{D}O_2I = CI \times CaO_2 \times 10$	
Oxygen extraction ratio	O_2ER	25%	Amount of oxygen extracted and consumed by the body tissues relative to the amount of oxygen delivered (Indicator of O_2 supply/demand)	$O_2ER = \dot{V}O_2/\dot{D}O_2 \times 100$ $= \dfrac{Ca - \bar{v}O_2 \times CO}{CaO_2 \times CO}$	2-7
Oxygen demand	$\dot{V}O_2$	See O_2 consumption			

Parameters

Parameter	Abbrev. or Symbol	Normal Values	Definition	Derivation Equation	Ref. Page #
Oxygen Index	OI	20-25 = mortality > 50% > 40 = high mortality		$OI = \dfrac{Paw \times FiO_2 \times 100}{PaO_2}$	
Oxygen reserve		750 ml/min	Venous oxygen supply		2-7
Oxygen saturation — arterial mixed venous venous	SaO_2 SvO_2 SvO_2	~ 95% - 100% ~ 75% (68-77%) Variable	Percent of total hemoglobin combined with oxygen	$SvO_2 = SaO_2 - Sa - \bar{v}O_2$	3-8
Oxygen supply	DO_2	See O_2 delivery			
Oxygen tension (pressure) — arterial mixed venous venous @ 50% saturation	PaO_2 PvO_2 PvO_2 P_{50}	Adult: 27 mmHg Fetal: 22 mmHg	See arterial oxygen tension See mixed venous oxygen tension See venous oxygen tension		
Oxygen transport	DO_2	See O_2 delivery			
Oxygen utilization coefficient	OUC		See oxygen extraction ratio		

Parameter	Abbrev. or Symbol	Normal Values	Definition	Derivation Equation	Ref. Page #
Physiologic shunt	$\dot{Q}s/\dot{Q}t$	< 0.05 (< 5%)	Percent of CO which passes from RA to LA without being oxygenated (Indicator of the efficiency of the pulmonary system)	$\dot{Q}s/\dot{Q}t = \dfrac{CcO_2 - CaO_2}{CcO_2 - CvO_2}$ or $\dot{Q}s/\dot{Q}t = \dfrac{A\text{-}aDO_2 \times 0.003}{Ca\text{-}vO_2 + A\text{-}aDO_2 \times 0.003}$	2-29
Preload Right ventricle or Left ventricle			Myocardial fiber length at end diastole (approximated by EDV or EDP)		
Pulmonary artery occlusion pressure	PAOP	See PAWP			
Pulmonary artery pressure: diastolic	PAP PADP	 8-15 mmHg	Blood pressure in the pulmonary artery Pressure in PA during diastolic phase of heartbeat (usually reported as end-diastolic)		7-3 7-18
end diastolic	PAEDP	0-12 mmHg	PADP at very end of diastolic phase (lowest pressure) (reflects filling pressure to LV)		

Parameter	Abbrev. or Symbol	Normal Values	Definition	Derivation Equation	Ref. Page #
mean	PAMP or $\overline{PAP}$	10-15 mmHg	Time averaged PA pressure	$PAMP = PASP + \dfrac{PASP + 2\ PADP}{3}$	
systolic	PASP or PA sys	15-25 mmHg	Pressure in PA during systole		7-18
Pulmonary artery wedge pressure	PAWP	4-12 mmHg	Mean blood pressure in the pulmonary capillaries (approximates LAP & LVEDP)		
Pulmonary capillary wedge pressure	PCWP	See pulmonary artery wedge pressure			
Pulmonary vascular resistance	PVR	20-250 dynes·sec·cm^{-5} (0.25-2.5 mmHg/L/min)	Resistance to RV ejection of blood into pulmonary vasculature (measure of RV afterload)	$PVR = \dfrac{(PAMP - PAWP) \times 80}{CO}$	2-44
Pulmonary vascular resistance index	PVRI	30-350 dynes·sec·cm^{-5}/m^{2}	Resistance to RV ejection into pulmonary vasculature per body surface area	$PVRI = PVR/BSA = \dfrac{(PAMP - PAWP) \times 80}{CI}$	
Pulse pressure	PP	40 mmHg (20-80 mmHg)	Difference in arterial BP between systolic and diastolic	$PP = BP\ sys - BP\ dia$	2-21 5-20 5-22

Parameter	Abbrev. or Symbol	Normal Values	Definition	Derivation Equation	Ref. Page #
Rate pressure product	RPP	< 12,000 mmHg/min	Indirect determinant of $M\dot{V}O_2$	RPP = BP sys × HR	
Right atrial pressure	RAP or RAP	0-6 mmHg	Mean pressure in right atrium (approximates CVP)		2-10
Right ventricular end diastolic pressure	RVEDP	0-5 mmHg	Blood pressure in RV at end diastole (reflects RV preload)		2-10
Right ventricular end diastolic volume	RVEDV	Can't measure clinically	Volume of blood in RV at end diastole		
Right ventricular end systolic pressure	RVESP	15-25 mmHg	Blood pressure in RV at end systole (reflects RV afterload)		2-10
Right ventricular end systolic volume	RVESV	Can't measure clinically	Volume of blood in RV at end systole		
Right ventricular stroke work	RVSW	10-15 gm/m/beat	Work performed by RV (measure of RV performance)	RVSW = SV × (PAMP − CVP) × 0.0136	2-26
Right ventricular stroke work index	RVSWI	4-12 gm/m/beat/m²	Work performed by RV per body surface area (indicator of RV contractility)	RVSWI = RVSW/BSA = SVI × (PAMP − CVP) × 0.0136	2-26 2-36
Shunt		See physiologic shunt			

Parameter	Abbrev. or Symbol	Normal Values	Definition	Derivation Equation	Ref. Page #
Stroke volume	SV	60-120 mL/beat	Amount of blood ejected by either ventricle per contraction	$SV = CO/HR \times 1000$ $SV = EDV - ESV$	2-26
Stroke volume index	SVI	35-75 ml/beat/m²	Amount of blood ejected by either ventricle per contraction per body surface area	$SVI = SV/BSA$ $SVI = CI/HR \times 1000$	
Stroke work	SW	See LVSW and RVSW	Measure of ventricle performance (how hard it works to eject blood)		2-26
Stroke work index	SWI	See LVSWI and RVSWI	Measure of ventricular performance per body surface area	$SWI = SW/BSA$	2-26
Systemic vascular resistance	SVR	800-1600 dynes·sec·cm⁻⁵ (10-20 mmHg / L / min)	Resistance to LV ejection of blood into systemic circulation (measure of LV afterload)	$SVR = \dfrac{BP - CVP}{CO} \times 80$	2-39
Systemic vascular resistance index	SVRI	1400-2600 dynes·sec·cm⁻⁵/m²	Resistance to LV ejection of blood into systemic circulation per body surface area (measure of LV afterload)	$SVRI = SVR/BSA$ $SVRI = \dfrac{(BP - CVP)}{CI} \times 80$	
Transmural pressure	PTM		Intravascular or intracardiac	$PTM = PIV - PIT$	7-36
Venous carbon dioxide tension (pressure)	PvCO₂	Varies with regional flow	(See mixed venous carbon dioxide tension)		

Parameters

Parameter	Abbrev. or Symbol	Normal Values	Definition	Derivation Equation	Ref. Page #
Venous hydrogen ion concentration	pHv	Varies with regional flow	(See mixed venous hydrogen ion concentration)		
Venous oxygen content	CvO_2	Varies with regional flow	(See mixed venous O_2 content)		
Venous oxygen saturation	SvO_2	Varies with regional flow	(See mixed venous O_2 sat)		
Venous oxygen tension (pressure)	PvO_2	Varies with regional flow	(See mixed venous O_2 tension)		
Venous pressure		See blood pressure or central venous pressure			
Ventricular end diastolic pressure	VEDP	See LVEDP and/or RVEDP			
Ventricular end diastolic volume	VEDV	See LVEDV and/or RVEDV			
Ventricular end systolic pressure	VESP	See LVESP and/or RVESP			
Ventricular end systolic volume	VESV	See LVESV and/or RVESV			

HEMODYNAMIC MONITORING PARAMETERS
Non-invasive vs. Invasive

NON-INVASIVE		INVASIVE*	
Measured	**Derived**	**Measured (Implied)**	**Derived**
BP (dia, sys)	$\overline{BP}$	BP dia, sys	$A\text{-}aDO_2$
Capillary refill	PP	CO	$a\text{-}vDO_2$
HR (pulse)	RPP	CVP	$a\text{-}\bar{v}DO_2$
LOC		HR	$\overline{BP}$
$P_{TC}CO_2$		$PaCO_2$	CaO_2
$P_{TC}O_2$		PaO_2	$Ca\text{-}vO_2$
RR		PADP	$Ca\text{-}\bar{v}O_2$
SaO_2		PASP	CI
Skin color/dryness		PAWP (LAP, LVEDP)	CPP
Temp (core & skin)		pH	CvO_2
UO		$PvCO_2$	$C\bar{v}O_2$
		$P\bar{v}CO_2$	$\dot{D}O_2$
Note: Non-invasive		PvO_2	LV function curve
parameters are valuable		$P\bar{v}O_2$	LVSW
assessment tools and		RAP (RVEDP)	LVSWI
should be noted every		SaO_2	$M\dot{D}O_2$
time any hemodynamic		SvO_2	$M\dot{V}O_2$
assessment is made.		$S\bar{v}O_2$	O_2ER
			PAMP
Although they are		*Many of these	PP
valuable indicators of a		parameters are	PVR
patient's status, many are		now being mea-	PVRI
slow or late indicators		sured or derived	$\dot{Q}s/\dot{Q}_T$
of change (especially in		non-invasively	RPP
the critically ill patient),		with varying	RVSW
and hence may be		degress of	RVSWI
misleading.		accuracy - see	SV
		pg 8-2	SVI
Also, non-invasive			SVR
parameter changes			SVRI
may often lag behind			SW
the correction of			SWI
physiological defects.			$\dot{V}O_2$
		NOTE: Invasive parameters offer up-to-date, minute-by-minute assessment of status and/or change.	

HEMODYNAMIC MONITORING PARAMETERS

Available per Invasive Lines

A-LINE		CVP LINE		PA LINE (THERMODILUTION)	
Measured	**Derived**	**Measured (Implied)**	**Derived**	**Measured (Implied)**	**Derived**
BP dia, sys	$A-aDO_2$	CVP	CvO_2	CO	CI
HR	$\overline{BP}$	HR		CVP	CvO_2
$PaCO_2$	CaO_2	pHv		HR	$Cv\overline{O_2}$
PaO_2	PP	$PvCO_2$		PADP	LV function curve
pHa	RPP	PvO_2		PASP	
SaO_2	SaO_2	RAP (RVEDP)		PAWP (LAP, LVEDP)	LVSW
		SvO_2		pHv	LVSWI
				$pH\overline{v}$	PAMP
				$PvCO_2$	PVR
		NOTE: All CVP line parameters may		$Pv\overline{CO_2}$	PVRI
		be obtained with the proximal		PvO_2	RVSW
		port of PA line.		$Pv\overline{O_2}$	RVSWI
				RAP (RVEDP)	SV
				SvO_2	SVI
				$Sv\overline{O_2}$	SW
					SWI

NOTE: All invasive parameters may be obtained with the combination of an A-line and a PA line (thermodil).

Derived

$a-vDO_2$	$M\dot{D}O_2$
$a-\overline{v}DO_2$	$M\dot{V}O_2$
$Ca-vO_2$	O_2ER
$Ca-\overline{v}O_2$	$\dot{Q}s/\dot{Q}T$
CPP	SVR
$\dot{D}O_2$	SVRI
	$\dot{V}O_2$

A-line parameters
+
PA line parameters

Chapter Contents

Physiology

(continued on next page)

CARDIOPULMONARY SYSTEM

Main Function: O_2 delivery (see next page)

Main Purpose: Adequate tissue perfusion—to deliver (supply) adequate O_2 and nutrients and remove metabolic wastes at a rate equal to the need (demand). (Maintain O_2 supply-demand balance.) (see page 2-6)

Main Goal: Tissue oxygenation (see page 2-5,7)

Physiology

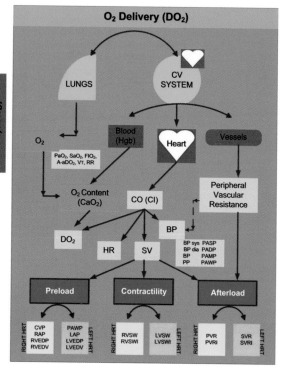

CARDIOPULMONARY SYSTEM'S MAIN PURPOSE: ADEQUATE TISSUE PERFUSION

Clinical Parameters for Assessing Tissue Perfusion	
Parameter	**Signs of ↓ Perfusion**
Arterial pulses	↓
Capillary refill	↓ (↑ time)
HR	↑
LOC	↓ ①
PP	↓ ④
RR	↓
Skin color	Δ ②
Skin temp	↓ ②
UO	↓ ③

① The brain is a sensitive indicator of tissue perfusion (O_2 supply). Early signs of underperfusion of the brain are apprehension, decreased short-term memory, inability to think abstractly, irritability, restlessness, uncooperativeness.

② Decreased skin color (pale) and decreased skin temp (cool) are indicative of ↓ perfusion to that area. Changes usually begin peripherally then move centrally as the CV status deteriorates. Cyanosis possible, but unreliable sign.

③ Urine output is a very sensitive indicator of acute changes in perfusion (when not receiving a diuretic). Decreased UO may occur long before other signs of impaired perfusion.

④ ↑ if due to aortic insufficiency.

CARDIOPULMONARY SYSTEM'S MAIN GOAL: TISSUE OXYGENATION

Definitions

O_2 Supply		
O_2 Delivery ($\dot{D}O_2$)	=	O_2 transport
	=	Quantity of O_2 pumped by the heart to body tissues per unit time (minute).

O_2 Demand		
O_2 Consumption ($\dot{V}O_2$)	=	Quantity of O_2 utilized by body tissues per unit time (minute).

O_2 Reserve		
Venous O_2 Supply	=	O_2 supply minus O_2 demand.

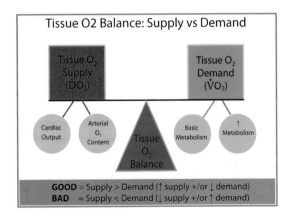

Tissue O2 Balance: Supply vs Demand

Tissue O_2 Supply (DO_2)

Tissue O_2 Demand ($\dot{V}O_2$)

Cardiac Output | Arterial O_2 Content | Tissue O_2 Balance | Basic Metabolism | ↑ Metabolism

GOOD = Supply > Demand (↑ supply +/or ↓ demand)
BAD = Supply < Demand (↓ supply +/or ↑ demand)

TISSUE OXYGENATION EQUATIONS

→ A - a DO_2 = P_AO_2 - PaO_2 **(A)**

Arterial O_2 supply = O_2 delivery ($\dot{D}O_2$) (O_2 transport)

$\dot{D}O2$ = Content arterial O_2 × cardiac output

= CaO_2 × CO × 10

(B) normal $\dot{D}O_2$ = 1000 ml/min

O_2 extraction ratio (O_2 ER) =
O_2 consumption (demand)
O_2 delivery (supply)

$O_2ER = \dfrac{\dot{V}O_2}{\dot{D}O_2}$ × 100

(D) Normal O_2ER = 25%

O_2 consumption ($\dot{V}O_2$) (O_2 demand)

$\dot{V}O_2$ = Fick equation

= arterial O_2 supply - venous reserve

= (CaO_2 × CO) - ($C\bar{v}O_2$ × CO) × 10

= Ca - $\bar{v}O_2$ × CO × 10

(C) normal $\dot{V}O_2$ = 250 ml/min

O_2 reserve = venous O_2 supply

O_2 reserve = $\dot{D}O_2$ - $\dot{V}O_2$

= content mixed venous
× cardiac output

= $C\bar{v}O_2$ × CO × 10

(E) Normal O_2 reserve = 750 ml/min

A-E (see next page)

2-7

EXAMPLES

A) $A\text{-}aDO_2$ $= PAO_2 - PaO_2$

$= [(P_B - PH_2O) FIO_2 - (PaCO_2 \times 1.25)] - PaO_2$

$= [(760 - 47) .21 - (40 \times 1.25)] - 95$

$= [100] - 95$

$= 5$ mmHg

B) $\dot{D}O_2$ $= CaO_2 \times CO \times 10$

$= [(SaO_2① \times Hgb② \times 1.36③) + (PaO_2 \times 0.0031④)] \times CO⑤ \times 10⑥$

$= [(0.98 \times 15$ gm/dl $\times 1.36) + (100 \times 0.0031)] \times 5$ L/m $\times 10$

$= [20$ vol (ml/dl) %] $\times 5$ L/m $\times 10$

$= 1000$ ml/min

C) $\dot{V}O_2$ $= (CaO_2 - C\bar{v}O_2⑦) \times CO \times 10$

$= (20$ vol %⑧$- 15$ vol %⑧$) \times 5$ L/m $\times 10⑤$

$= 5$ vol % $\times 5$ L/m $\times 10$

$= 250$ ml/min

D) O_2ER $= \dfrac{\dot{V}O_2}{\dot{D}O_2} \times 100$

$= \dfrac{(CaO_2 - C\bar{v}O_2) \times CO \times 10}{CaO_2 \times CO \times 10}$

$= \dfrac{250 \text{ ml/min}ⒸⒸ}{1000 \text{ ml/min}Ⓑ}$

$= 25\%$

E) O_2 Reserve

$= \dot{D}O_2 - \dot{V}O_2 = 1000$ ml/min $- 250$ ml/min $= 750$ ml/min or

$= C\bar{v}O_2⑦ \times CO \times 10$

$= [(S\bar{v}O_2① \times Hgb② \times 1.36③) + (P\bar{v}O_2 \times 0.0031④)] \times CO⑤ \times 10⑥$

$= [(0.75 \times 15$ gm/dl $\times 1.36) + (40 \times 0.0031)] \times 5$ L/m $\times 10$

$= [15$ vol (ml/dl) %] $\times 5$ L/m $\times 10$

$= 750$ ml/min

① $SaO_2 + S\bar{v}O_2$ may be used for clinical estimates of CaO_2 and $C\bar{v}O_2$, respectively. Estimates may vary by 25% or more.

② Hgb = gm/dl

③ Number of ml of O_2 each gram of Hgb can carry. Some equations employ 1.34.

④ mlO_2/mmHg PaO_2. Often clinically ignored due to small amount.

⑤ CO may be calculated by Fick equation, see page 8-7.

⑥ 10 is the conversion factor of Hgb (gm/dl) to gm/1000 ml.

⑦ CvO_2 may be substituted for $C\bar{v}O_2$ if a PA sample not available.

O₂ SUPPLY/DEMAND REGULATION

Response to Increased Tissue O_2 Demands in Various Bodily States

Compensatory Mechanism	Normal Body Function	Cardiopulmonary Dysfunction	Cardiopulmonary Failure
1st Response: ↑ O_2 supply [1] (↑HR, ↑CO, ↑RR, ↑SV)	Greatest source of compensation— Normal patients can increase O_2 supply (ie: ↑ CO) at least 3x normal (↑ supply generally meets all demands)	Limited compensation due to defective supply system (i.e., CO, Sat, Hgb)	No or extremely limited compensation due to defective supply system (patient may not even be able to meet resting demands)
2nd Response: ↓ O_2 reserve	When demand is excessive and begins to exceed supply. Normally the O_2 reserve may be used up down to 30% sat (approx. 3x normal extraction). Hence, a normal patient can meet a 9x increase in O_2 demand (3 x CO x 3 x reserve) before resorting to the 3rd level of response. (Obviously, any defects in normal compensatory mechanisms will limit this ability.)	The 2nd and 3rd response mechanisms become the major source of compensation	Quickly depleted (3-4 minutes of O_2 supply stops completely, i.e., arrest)
3rd Response: Anaerobic metabolism	When tissue demand exceeds supply and reserve (e.g., strenuous exercise).		The only source of compensation [2]

[1] See chart on Pg. 3-11 for specific regulatory mechanisms.

[2] Anaerobic metabolism $\rightarrow$ 20x less energy $\searrow$ ↓ cell function $\rightarrow$ eventual cell death

$\nearrow$ ↑ lactic acid $\nearrow$ ↓ CV function

Physiology

PULMONARY ARTERY:
SYSTOLIC 15-25 mmHg
DIASTOLIC 8-15 mmHg
MEAN 10-15 mmHg

20 —
15 —
10 —
5 —

DIASTOLE SYSTOLE DIASTOLE

R

ECG

P   T   P

PULMONARY WEDGE
MEAN 4-12 mmHg

10 —
5 —

DIASTOLE SYSTOLE DIASTOLE

R

ECG

P   T   P

R. ATRIUM:
MEAN 0-6 mmHg

5 —
0 —

DIASTOLE SYSTOLE DIASTOLE

R

ECG

P   T   P

R. VENTRICLE
SYSTOLIC 15-25 mmHg
DIASTOLIC 0-6 mmHg

25 —
20 —
15 —
10 —
5 —

DIASTOLE SYSTOLE DIASTOLE

R

ECG

P   T   P

— 15
0

RIGHT   RIGHT   PULMONARY   WEDGE
ATRIUM   VENTRICLE   ARTERY   PRESSURE

2-10

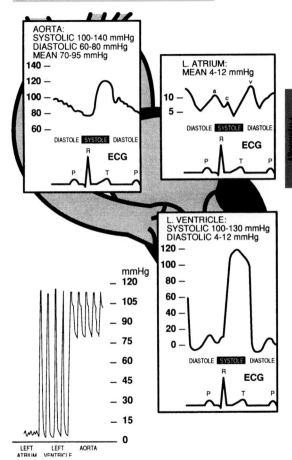

HEART PRESSURE WAVEFORMS

NAME/ABBREV.	WAVEFORM	DESCRIPTION
Right Atrial Pressure (RAP) (CVP)		a wave = pressure rise during atrial systole (occurs at time of P-R interval) x descent = pressure fall during atrial relaxation c wave = slight pressure rise due to bulging of A-V valve during ventricular systole (may distort the x-descent as a notch, a separate wave or may be absent) v wave = pressure rises due to venous inflow into atria while A-V valves are closed (occurs at time of T-P interval) y descent = pressure fall during passive atrial emptying
Left Atrial Pressure (LAP)		Same as RAP waveform with slightly higher amplitude Note: PAWP waveform is very similar to the atrial waveform, except usually no c wave
Right Ventricular Pressure (RVP + RVEDP)		Same as LVP waveform except 1/5 the amplitude (Pressure)
Left Ventricular Pressure (LVP + LVEDP)		a wave = pressure rise during atrial systole. "Plateau" immediately following "a" wave = LVEDP. Vertical upstroke = pressure rise during isovolumetric contraction (see Pg. 2-14). Downward slope = pressure fall during rapid ejection, prodiastolic and isovolumetric relaxation phases. (See Pg. 2-14, 15); Bottom of wave = passive filling phase of ventricle

CARDIAC CYCLE WITH PRESSURE WAVEFORMS & HEART SOUNDS

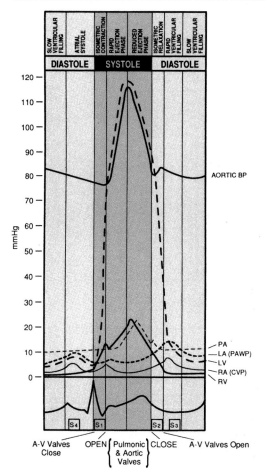

2-13

CARDIAC CYCLE

PHASE	HEART SOUND	EVENTS
Ventricular Systole (Ventricles emptying)	S_1	Ventricles contract, pressure rises
		A-V valves close (mitral and tricuspid)
		Pressure continues to rise, volume remains the same
		ECG: Peak R wave
Isovolumetric contraction		
Rapid ventricular ejection		Pulmonary and aortic valves open as ventricular pressures exceed 8 mmHg and 80 mmHg, respectively (diastolic pressure)
		Blood is pushed into pulmonary artery and aorta by RH and LH, respectively
		Ventricular pressures continue to rise to peak
		LV 120 mmHg (BP sys)
		RV 20-25 mmHg (PASP)
		ECG: ST segment
Prodiastole (Reduced ejection)	S_2	Ventricular pressures fall and outflow slows and stops
		Blood flow in arteries reverses and begins to flow back towards heart
		(Dicrotic notches in waveforms occur)
		Pulmonary and aortic valves close

2-14

CARDIAC CYCLE

PHASE		HEART SOUND	EVENTS
Ventricular Diastole (Ventricles filling)			Ventricles relax and ventricular pressures fall until pressures in ventricles become less than atrial pressures
			All valves are closed
	Isovolumetric relaxation		
	Passive filling (Early diastole) Diastasis	S_3 (ventricular gallop)	A-V valves open
			Atria passively empty into the ventricles
			Ventricles fill (up to 70–90%)
			(S3 usually only occurs with ↓ compliance of heart wall)
			ECG: P wave
Atrial systole (atrial kick)		S_4 (atrial gallop)	This phase begins with peak of P wave
			Atria contract and push remaining blood into ventricles
			Ventricles fill (to 100%)
			(S4 usually only occurs with vigorous atrial systole or if there is resistance to filling)
End diastole			Period just prior to ventricular systole = end diastolic volume and point at which VEDP is measured (LVEDP, LAP, PAWP, and RAP, RVEDP)

2-15

MYOCARDIAL OXYGENATION

CLINICAL NOTE

Optimal CO is dependent on adequate myocardial tissue O_2:

Adequate myocardial tissue O_2 = O_2 supply ≥ O_2 demand

Myocardial O_2 Supply	**Myocardial O_2 Demand**
Myocardial O_2 delivery ($M\dot{D}O_2$) =	Myocardial O_2 consumption ($M\dot{V}O_2$) =
O_2 transport to myocardium	O_2 utilized by myocardium

Myocardial O_2 Reserve =
O_2 supply minus O_2 demand
= essentially zero ①

①

All myocardial demand <u>must</u> be met by CBF (O_2 supply) because:
1. There are no O_2 reserves in myocardial muscle
2. The LV extracts 70% of all O_2 flowing through it

Hence an ↑ in myocardial demand must be matched by an ↑ in CBF (supply).

**FACTORS DETERMINING
MYOCARDIAL O_2 SUPPLY/DEMAND**

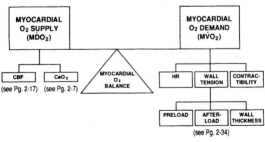

Adapted from Daily, E.K. and Schroeder, J.S., *Techniques in Bedside Hemodynamic Monitoring,* 4th Ed. Copyright 1989 by C.V. Mosby Co., St. Louis.

MYOCARDIAL O₂ SUPPLY (MḊO₂)

Coronary Blood Flow (CBF)		
Factors determining	**Normal physiology**	**Physiological Δ /Pathology**
Flow resistance	Vessel compression: 75% of perfusion occurs during diastole. Flow ↓ during systole due to compression as heart contracts. * Hence duration of diastole becomes a critical factor in CBF/perfusion	Autoregulation maintains a normal CBF within a BP range of 60–80 mmHg. Autoregulation is determined primarily by O_2 ($\downarrow O_2 \rightarrow$ vasodilation in coronary vessels) The precise roles of other factors (sympathetic nerves, metabolic byproducts, etc.) are yet to be determined. ↑ HR → ↓ diastolic time → ↓ CBF
Pressure gradient	Pressure gradient = Coronary perfusion pressure (CPP) CPP = aortic diastolic pressure — coronary venous pressure = BP dia – LVEDP	↑ BP dia: exercise, vasoconstriction drugs, ↑ SVR, IABP ↓ BP dia: shock, hypovolemia, aortic regurgitation ↑ LVEDP: acute MI, CHF

Physiology

CLINICAL ESTIMATE OF CBF

CPP = BP dia − PAWP

CPP normal range = 60-80 mmHg

> 80 mmHg → ↓ CBF due to reflex vasoconstriction

< 60 mmHg → usually inadequate perfusion especially if ↑HR or acute MI

< 40 mmHg → collapse of coronary vessels (↓ CBF)

CLINICAL NOTE

Inadequate coronary perfusion may exist even with a normal $\overline{BP}$ or BP dia., if ↑ PAWP.

(Ex. CPP = BP dia − PAWP = 75 − 25 = 50)

Myocardial O₂ Demand

(O₂ Consumption, $M\dot{v}O_2$)

$M\dot{v}O_2$ Normal Range = 8 − 15 ml O_2/min/100 gm LV

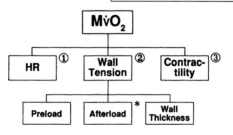

①, ②, ③ and *—see next page.

①	$\uparrow$ HR $\rightarrow$ $\uparrow$ # contractions/time $\rightarrow$	$\uparrow$ M$\dot{V}O_2$
	$\uparrow$ HR $\rightarrow$ $\uparrow$ contractility $\rightarrow$	$\uparrow$ M$\dot{V}O_2$
	$\uparrow$ HR $\rightarrow$ $\downarrow$ EDV $\rightarrow$ $\downarrow$ wall tension $\rightarrow$	$\downarrow$ M$\dot{V}O_2$
		may balance out?

② $\uparrow$ wall tension $\rightarrow$ $\uparrow$ M$\dot{V}O_2$

> tension = $\dfrac{\text{BP sys} \times \text{vent. radius}}{\text{Wall Thickness}}$
>
> (Law of LaPlace)

* Afterload (pressure work of heart):
  Most important determinant of M$\dot{V}O_2$
     $\uparrow$ afterload $\rightarrow$ $\uparrow$ BP sys $\rightarrow$ $\uparrow$ work $\rightarrow$ $\uparrow$ wall tension

  Preload: $\uparrow$ preload $\rightarrow$ $\uparrow$ EDV $\rightarrow$ $\uparrow$ vent size $\rightarrow$ $\uparrow$ wall tension

  Wall thickness: $\uparrow$ hypertrophy $\rightarrow$ $\downarrow$ wall tension

③ $\uparrow$ contractility $\rightarrow$ $\uparrow$ M$\dot{V}O_2$
     Contractility is assessed by ventricular function curves
     (see Pg 2-36)

M$\dot{V}O_2$ $\approx$ cardiac work
   $\approx$ external work[①] + internal work[②]
   $\approx$ stroke work[③]
   $\approx$ volume - pressure work
   $\approx$ SV x P generated by ventricle[④]

①   External work = energy used to eject blood against afterload.
②   Internal work = energy wasted in heat production/cell metabolism. This is not clinically quantified.
③   Stroke work (SW) x HR = minute work.
④   Estimate of SW $\approx$ CO x $\overline{BP}$ (SV x P generated).

> **Clinical estimate of relative myocardial O_2 consumption**
> $$M\dot{V}O_2 \approx CO \times \overline{BP}$$
> or
> $$HR \times \overline{BP}$$

$$BP = CO \times SVR$$

Cardiac Output

Volume of blood ejected from LV into aorta per minute
(RV output = LV output, unless intracardiac shunt)
HR x SV (# systoles/min x volume ejected/systole)

normal CO = 72 beats/min x 65 ml = 4680 ml/min
= 4 – 8 L/m (avg = 5 L/m, (4.75 female, 5.60 male)

Cardiac Index (CI):

CI = CO/BSA (CO in relation to body size)
  = Greater clinical value than CO, a more precise
      indicator of circulatory status and tissue perfusion.

Normal CI = 2.5 – 4.2 $L/min/m^2$

VARIATIONS IN CI

CI ≥ 2.2 ≈ good cardiac function (favorable cardiac prognosis)

CI 1.8 – 2.1 ≈ moderate cardiac depression
            (Impending deterioration)
            Treatment usually effective

CI ≤ 1.7 ≈ severe cardiac depression
          (Poor prognosis)
          Demands immediate and effective treatment

↑ CI	↓ CI
Exercise	abnormal HR
Mild	
tachy-arrhythmia	abnormal preload:
Sepsis	↓ preload → ↓ SV → ↓ CO
↓ afterload	↑ preload (beyond Starling limit) → ↓ SV → ↓ CO
	↑ afterload
	↓ contractility

Systemic Vascular Resistance — see Pg. 2-39.

Physiology

ARTERIAL BLOOD PRESSURES

Pressure	Abbrev.	Normal Values (Range)	Definition	Clinical Note
BP systolic	BP sys	120mmHg (100-140 mmHg)	Highest pressure in artery during cardiac cycle	Primarily determined by LV pressure (in absence of aortic stenosis) and also by SVR. BP sys increases distal to heart (eg: femoral BP sys = 20-50 mmHg > brachial BP sys, but BP is unchanged)
BP diastolic	BP dia	80 mmHg (60-80 mmHg)	Lowest pressure in artery during cardiac cycle	Primarily determined by the vasodilation/constriction of arterioles (SVR) and also elasticity of arterial system and HR
Pulse Pressure	PP	40 mmHg (20-80 mmHg)	BP sys - BP dia	Primarily determined by SV and aortic elasticity (PP ≈ SV, ↓ PP by 50% ≈ ↓ SV by 50%)
Mean arterial pressure	$\overline{BP}$ (MAP)	93 mmHg (70-105 mmHg)	Average pressure in artery during cardiac cycle (avg driving press to systemic circ) $$\frac{BP\ sys + 2\ BP\ dia\ ①}{3}$$ $$\boxed{BP = CO \times SVR}$$ $$\boxed{BP - RAP = CO \times SVR}$$	Primarily determined by CO and SVR ① The clinical equation becomes less accurate when HR > 120 because BP dia is < 2x as long as BP sys

2-21

ARTERIAL BLOOD PRESSURE WAVEFORM
(See also Pg 5-21)

Waveform	Description / Note
	**Anacrotic Limb:** **Upstroke** = pressure rise due to blood entering vessel from ventricular ejection Slope (rate of rise) ≈ speed of ventricular emptying Fast upstroke = aortic regurgitation or hyperdynamic heart Slowed upstroke = aortic stenosis or V failure **Dicrotic Limb:** **Downstroke** = pressure falls due to blood run-off into capillaries and veins. **Dicrotic notch** = closure of aortic semilunar valve. As blood progresses distally towards peripheral vessels, the form and amplitude changes: (See Pg. 5-21) ↑ BP sys, waveform narrows, rises more sharply, dicrotic notch diminishes

BP regulation =   CO regulation (see Pg 2-24)
                    +
                    SVR regulation (see Pg 2-40)

OVERVIEW

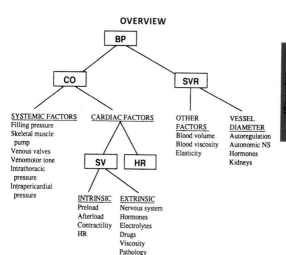

Physiology

CARDIAC OUTPUT REGULATION

Factors	Definition	Description/Notes
Systemic factors (affects blood return to heart) Systemic filling pressure (SFP)	Force "pushing" blood into RA	SFP ≈ venous return volume (should equal CO) = Driving force (of LV) from LV to RA. Normal SFP = 7 mmHg $$\text{Net SFP} = \text{SFP} - \text{RAP}$$ $$= 7 - 0$$ $$= 7$$
Skeletal muscle pump	Rhythmic contractions of muscles in lower extremities	↑ contractions (eg. exercise) → ↓ venous return
Venous valves	Promote unidirectional flow of venous return	↓ competency → ↓ venous return
Venomotor tone	Dilation/constriction of venous vessels by neural and humoral stimuli or drugs	↑ venotone (constriction) → ↑ venous return
Intrathoracic pressure	Pressure in thoracic cavity	Negative pressure (ie: spontaneous inspiration) improves venous return Positive pressure (spontaneous expiration, PPV and/or PEEP) decreases venous return
Intrapericardial pressure	Pressure around outside of heart	↑ pressure (esp. cardiac tamponade) → ↓ filling of heart (↓ venous return)

Factors	Definition	Description/Notes
Cardiac Factors (affects blood ejection)		HR is: **A major determinant of CO:** Most rapid and effective way to Δ CO. Can increase CO 2 – 3X. More important than SV in making major temporary adjustments in CO.
Heart Rate (HR)	Frequency of contraction	**A major determinant of SV:** $\downarrow$ HR $\rightarrow$ $\uparrow$ diastolic time $\rightarrow$ $\uparrow$ vent filling $\rightarrow$ $\uparrow$ preload $\rightarrow$ $\uparrow$ SV $\rightarrow$ $\uparrow$ CO
	CLINICAL NOTE HR is a major determinant of coronary perfusion and $M\dot{V}O_2$: $\downarrow$ HR $\diagdown$ $\uparrow$ diastolic time $\rightarrow$ $\uparrow$ perfusion $\rightarrow$ $\uparrow$ O_2 supply $\downarrow$ contractions $\rightarrow$ $\downarrow$ $M\dot{V}O_2$ $\rightarrow$ $\downarrow$ O_2 demand $\uparrow$ HR $\diagdown$ $\downarrow$ diastolic time $\rightarrow$ $\downarrow$ perfusion $\rightarrow$ $\downarrow$ O_2 supply $\uparrow$ contractions $\rightarrow$ $\uparrow$ $M\dot{V}O_2$ $\rightarrow$ $\uparrow$ O_2 demand	$\uparrow$ HR (>120) $\rightarrow$ $\downarrow$ diastolic time $\rightarrow$ $\downarrow$ vent filling $\rightarrow$ $\downarrow$ preload $\rightarrow$ $\downarrow$ SV $\rightarrow$ $\downarrow$ CO **NOTE** $\downarrow$ HR < 50 $\rightarrow$ $\downarrow$ CO (esp. with cardiac disease) $\uparrow$ HR > 120: Caution In hearts being artificially paced, CO will $\downarrow$ due to other factors not being increased. The heart of a young adult may be able to handle rates up to 180 without $\downarrow$ CO.
	HENCE HR > 100 – 120 is not advantageous for O_2 supply/ demand balance (especially in patient with cardiac disease)	

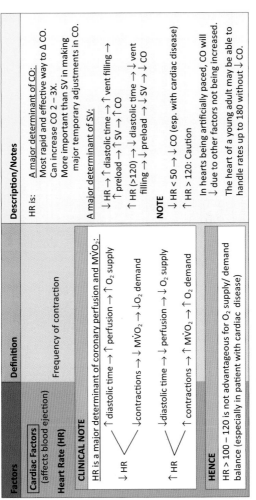

2-25

Factors	Definition	Description/Notes
Stroke Volume (SV)	Volume of blood ejected by ventricle with each contraction	SV = CO/HR SV = EDV − ESV Ejection fraction (EF) = SV/EDV norm EF = 0.5 − 0.75 (50-75%) EF < 50% = serious ventricular dysfunction EF < 35% = profound ventricular dysfunction Stroke Work (SW) ≈ performance of ventricles SW = SV × P generated by ventricle $LVSW = SV \times (\overline{BP} - PAWP) \times 0.0136$① $RVSW = SV \times (PAMP - CVP) \times 0.0136$ 0.0136 = Conversion Factor of pressure to work (mmHg/ml to gm/m/beat) Stroke Work Index = SW/BSA ① Some equations substitute BP sys and PA sys for $\overline{BP}$ and PAMP (PA) respectively.
	Normals LVSW = 60-80 gm/m/beat LVSWI = 40-75 gm/m/beat/m² RVSW = 10-15 gm/m/beat RVSWI = 4-12 gm/m/beat/m²	

Factors	Definition	Description/Notes
Stroke Volume, (cont.) Intrinsic: ① Preload	Inherent contractile properties Pressure or volume of blood in ventricle at end diastole	See Pg 2-29
Afterload	Total force opposing ventricular ejection	See Pg 2-34
Contractility	Contraction ability (independent of preload or afterload)	See Pg 2-36
Homeometric (autoregulation)	An improvement in ventricular performance without a Δ in fiber length	Has minimal clinical importance
Heart rate	Frequency and force of contraction	See Pg 2-25
Extrinsic: Neurohumoral effects	Autonomic nervous system and circulating catecholamines	Blood levels: K^+, Ca^{++}, pH
Chemical and/or pharmacological effects	Affects myocardial contractility and rhythm	Drugs: Digitalis, Ca^{++} antagonists, sympathetic blocking agents — anesthetics, etc.
Blood viscosity		Anemia $\rightarrow \downarrow$ SVR $\rightarrow \uparrow$ CO Polycythemia $\rightarrow \uparrow$ SVR $\rightarrow \downarrow$ CO
Pathological effects		Muscle damage: ischemia, bacteria, chemicals

① Although these represent separate mechanisms, they all are interrelated in their function.

2-27

SUMMARY OF CARDIAC REGULATION

CO = HR X SV		
Primary Alteration	**Results in:** and	**Compensatory Mechanism**
↓ HR	↓ CO	↑ SV
↑ HR	↑ CO	↓ SV
↑ SV	↑ CO	↓ HR
↓ SV	↓ CO	↑ HR

Classical Clinical Picture of Decreased CO		
↓ CO < 2 L/m	↑ SVR > 1500 dynes•sec•cm^{-5}	Peripheral vasoconstriction: cold, pale or cyanotic extremities
↓ PP < 30 mmHg	↓ LVSWI < 30 gm/m/beat/m^2	
↑ CVP	↓ UO < 30 mL/hr	↓ capillary refill
↑ PAWP > 15 mmHg	↑ urine Sp. gravity > 1.02	↑ metabolic acidosis

COMMON CAUSES OF DECREASED CO

Inadequate LV Filling

Arrhythmias
Cardiac tamponade
Constrictive pericarditis
Hypovolemia
Restrictive cardiomyopathy
Tachycardia
Shock
Valve stenosis
   (tricuspid, pulmonic, mitral)

Inadequate LV Ejection

Acute MI
Aortic valve stenosis
Cardiomyopathy
Hypertension
Myocardial ischemia
Myocarditis
Mitral regurgitation

PRELOAD

Definition
1. Length of muscle fibers at end-diastole.
2. Filling volume of blood in ventricle at end-diastole.
3. Filling pressure at end-diastole (clinical definition).
   VEDP ≈ VEDV ≈ fiber length
   These correlate well clinically only when normal myocardial compliance and normal juxtacardia pressure (see ventricular function curve, Pg. 2-31 and Pg. 2-33)

Values

Ventricle Pressure	Normal Values ①	Measured by:	
RVEDP	0-6 mmHg (0-8 cmH$_2$O)	RAP or CVP	(In normal heart with normal tricuspid valve)
LVEDP	4-12 mmHg ②	LAP, PAWP or PADP	(In normal heart with normal mitral valve and normal pulmonary vasculature)

① Clinical Value = VEDP
   True Value = transmural pressure (VEDP - pericardial pressure) (Pericardial pressure is usually negligible unless tamponade.)

② LVEDP = 15-18 is upper physiological limit for improved LV function.
   LVEDP > 15-18 is potential for ↓LV function and pulmonary congestion.
   LVEDP > 20 results in probable pulmonary congestion.
   LVEDP > 25 results in pulmonary edema.
   (Assuming normal myocardial compliance and juxtacardiac pressures)

CLINICAL NOTE

Optimal preload = peak myocardial performance (i.e., adequate
CO without pulmonary edema or worsening ischemia).

Starling's Law: ↑ preload → ↑ myocardial performance (up
to physiological limits) (> optimal → ↓ performance) (see
next page)

Peak performance — varies with patient and ventricle
compliance. Disease alters ventricle compliance:
  In sepsis or shock: optimal LV preload = 10-15 mmHg
  In acute MI: optimal LV preload = 18-24 mmHg

FACTORS DETERMINING PRELOAD

(End diastolic fiber length)

Factor	Comments
Atrial Kick	↑ atrial pressure → ↑ ventricular diastolic filling. Esp. important in patients with ↓ ventricular compliance (see Pg. 2-33)
Blood Volume: Total and distribution	Volume of venous return is affected by total intravascular volume (hemorrhage) and its distribution (body position, venous tone, intrathoracic pressure, etc.)
Filling Pressure	Function of atrial press (kick), blood volume and venous return
Heart Rate	Duration of diastole greatly affects filling time, and hence end-diastolic volume (↑ HR → ↓ filling time)

PRELOAD AND STROKE VOLUME

Starling's Law states that the more the heart is filled (preload), the greater the contractile force (SV) within physiological limits.

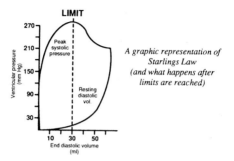

A graphic representation of Starlings Law (and what happens after limits are reached)

Ventricular Function Curve (Preload vs. Stroke Volume)

Ventricular performance can be assessed by the relation between preload (LVEDP) and stroke volume (CO).

A ventricular function curve can be constructed with any of the following parameters (use any one parameter/axis):

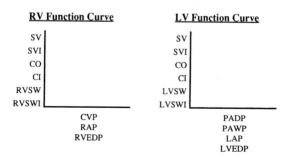

NOTE:

At any given moment, the ventricle operates on a particular curve. The curve may vary in shape from time to time as intrinsic and extrinsic factors change the functioning of the myocardium.

The plateau represents the physiological limits of Starling's Law.

When using SV or CO, the curve will shift with changes in afterload or contractility.

When using LVSW, the curve will shift only minimally with a change in afterload ($\uparrow$ afterload $\rightarrow$ $\uparrow$ BPsys + $\downarrow$ SV [effects cancel out]). Hence any shift can be attributed to a change in contractility.

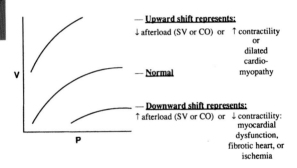

— <u>**Upward shift represents:**</u>

$\downarrow$ afterload (SV or CO) or $\uparrow$ contractility or dilated cardio-myopathy

— <u>**Normal**</u>

— <u>**Downward shift represents:**</u>

$\uparrow$ afterload (SV or CO) or $\downarrow$ contractility: myocardial dysfunction, fibrotic heart, or ischemia

Ventricular function curves can be used to determine optimal ventricular function and optimal PAWP by adjusting fluids, vasoactive and inotropic therapies.

Example:

$\uparrow$ PAWP (LVEDP) + $\downarrow$ SV (CO) may indicate left ventricular failure (LVF) prior to clinical manifestations.

[LVF $\rightarrow$ $\downarrow$ S V $\rightarrow$ $\uparrow$ LVEDV $\rightarrow$ $\uparrow$ LVEDP $\rightarrow$ $\uparrow$ PAWP]

PRELOAD AND VENTRICULAR COMPLIANCE

Relation of EDP to EDV is a function of ventricular compliance.

Normal Compliance (EDP ≈ EDV)

Large increases in EDV produce small increases in EDP (until higher volumes are reached).

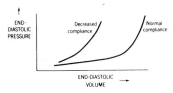

Altered Compliance (disease states)

Normal volume-pressure relationship is changed: (EDP ≠ EDV)

Increased compliance (ex. dilated cardiomyopathy)

Large ↑ EDV → smaller ↑ EDP

Decreased compliance (ex. PEEP, ischemia, acute fibrotic heart disease, etc.)

Small ↑ EDV → large ↑ EDP

CLINICAL NOTE

Normal LVEDP = 4-12 mmHg

< 12 mmHg may be inadequate in states of decreased compliance.

(↓ EDP → ↓ EDV → ↓ SV)

Altered ventricular compliance → altered ventricular function curve: Ex. ↓ compliance → ↑ EDP / ↓ EDV → ↓ SV (depressed curve)

PRELOAD AND M$\dot{V}O_2$

M$\dot{V}O_2$ ≈ preload (heart diameter) *

NOTE:

↑ preload 2X → ↑ M$\dot{V}O_2$ 2X

Hence, may ↓ M$\dot{V}O_2$ with diuretics and/or venodilators

---

* Insure proper balance between M$\dot{V}O_2$ and O_2 delivery (M$\dot{D}O_2$) to heart tissue.)

AFTERLOAD

Definition:

Total force opposing ventricular ejection.

Also defined as:

- Outflow impedance or pressure.
- The load the heart must move during contraction.
- Pressure the heart must develop before fibers can begin to shorten.

Reflects LV wall tension during systole.

Factors determining afterload:

1. Diastolic Pressure ($\uparrow$ pressure $\rightarrow$ $\uparrow$ afterload)

2. Resistance to flow ($\uparrow$ resistance $\rightarrow$ $\uparrow$ afterload)
   The primary determinant of resistance is arteriole wall tension (so . . . heart wall tension $\approx$ arteriole wall tension)

Values:

A true measure of afterload is difficult to obtain.
A clinical measure is provided by derived calculations of PVR and SVR. (See also Pgs. 2-39 and 2-44)

Clinical measure of afterload:

RV afterload = PADP + PVR ①
LV afterload = BP dia + SVR ②

① PVR = $\dfrac{\text{PAMP} - \text{PAWP}}{\text{CO}} \times 80$

② SVR = $\dfrac{\overline{\text{BP}} - \text{CVP}}{\text{CO}} \times 80$

Physiology

AFTERLOAD AND STROKE VOLUME

$$\text{Afterload} \approx 1/\text{SV}$$

> $\uparrow$ afterload $\rightarrow \downarrow$ SV
>
> $\downarrow$ afterload $\rightarrow \uparrow$ SV

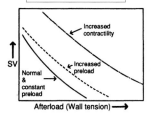

AFTERLOAD AND Mv̇O$_2$

$$\text{Mv̇O}_2 \approx \text{afterload*}$$

> $\uparrow$ afterload $\rightarrow \uparrow$ Mv̇O$_2$
>
> $\downarrow$ afterload $\rightarrow \downarrow$ Mv̇O$_2$

Afterload is the most important determinant of Mv̇O$_2$.

> Ex. $\uparrow$ SVR $\rightarrow \downarrow$ SV $\rightarrow \uparrow$ pressure work of heart to compensate $\rightarrow \uparrow$ Mv̇O$_2$
>
> $\downarrow$ SVR $\rightarrow \uparrow$ SV $\rightarrow \downarrow$ pressure work of heart needed $\rightarrow \downarrow$ Mv̇O$_2$

CLINICAL NOTE

"Unloading" of ventricle = $\downarrow$ afterload (ie, $\downarrow$ SVR with vasodilators)

* Insure proper balance between Mv̇O$_2$ and O$_2$ delivery (MḋO$_2$) to heart tissue.

Physiology

CONTRACTILITY

Definition:

Inotropic state of myocardium

Inherent ability to increase force of contraction independent of preload and afterload

Value:

No clinical measure is available

Its effect can be appreciated by changes in the ventricular function curve (see below and Pg. 2-31)

Contractility ≈ ventricular work (SWI)

RV contractility ≈ RVSWI
LV contractility ≈ LVSWI

CONTRACTILITY AND VENTRICULAR FUNCTION CURVES

| ↑ contractility | ↓ contractility |
(+ inotropes)	(− inotropes)
Steeper slope	Flattened slope
Upward shift	Downward shift

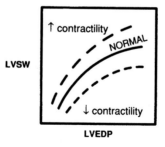

LVSW

↑ contractility

NORMAL

↓ contractility

LVEDP

Factors affecting contractility (when other determinants are constant)

Note: Changes in contractility are usually initiated by extrinsic factors.

↑ Contractility (↑ SV) (⊕ inotropic effect)	↓ Contractility (↓ SV) (⊖ inotropic effect)

⊕ Inotropic agents:
    Digitalis
    Amrinone (Inocor)
	Acidemia
	Anesthetic agents
	Antiarrhythmic agents
	    (most common):
	      Procainamide
	      Quinidine

Beta stimulant drugs:
    Dobutamine (Dobutrex)
    Dopamine (Intropin)
    Epinephrine ① (adrenalin)
    Isoproterenol ② (Isuprel)
    Norepinephrine (Levophed)
	Beta blocking agents:
	    Propanolol
	    etc.
	Ca channel blocking agents
	Hyperkalemia
	Hyponatremia

Hypercalcemia	Hypoxemia / Hypercapnia (severe)

Phosphodiesterase inhibitors:
    (↑ cyclic AMP):
    Amrinone ②
    Milrinone ②	

Sympathetic NS stimulation	Ischemia / Infarction

① Epinephrine, norepinephrine, and high-dose dopamine also cause peripheral vasconstriction (↑ SVR) and ↑ contractility to increase perfusion pressure.

② Also produce beta-2 stimulation in vascular smooth muscle → ↓ SVR.

CONTRACTILITY AND MV̇O₂

$$M\dot{V}O_2 \approx \text{Contractility} *$$

$$↑ \text{ contractility} → ↑ M\dot{V}O_2$$

$$↓ \text{ contractility} → ↓ M\dot{V}O_2$$

* Insure proper balance between $M\dot{V}O_2$ and O_2 delivery ($M\dot{D}O_2$) to heart tissue.

SUMMARY OF INTRINSIC STROKE VOLUME REGULATION

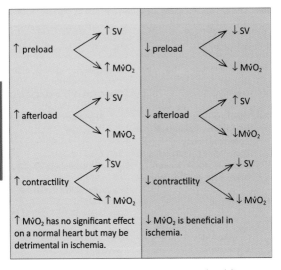

↑ preload ⟨ ↑ SV / ↑ Mv̇O₂

↓ preload ⟨ ↓ SV / ↓ Mv̇O₂

↑ afterload ⟨ ↓ SV / ↑ Mv̇O₂

↓ afterload ⟨ ↑ SV / ↓ Mv̇O₂

↑ contractility ⟨ ↑ SV / ↑ Mv̇O₂

↓ contractility ⟨ ↓ SV / ↓ Mv̇O₂

↑ Mv̇O₂ has no significant effect on a normal heart but may be detrimental in ischemia.

↓ Mv̇O₂ is beneficial in ischemia.

NOTE: Insure a proper balance between MV̇O₂ and O₂ delivery (ḊO₂) to tissues (SV).

SYSTEMIC VASCULAR RESISTANCE (SVR)

Definitions:

Force the LV must overcome to maintain systemic blood flow

Peripheral blood vessel resistance to blood flow

Value:

$$SVR = \frac{\overline{BP} - CVP}{CO} \times 80$$

Normal SVR = 800 – 1600 dynes•sec•cm^{-5}
or
= 10–20 units (mmHg/L/min)

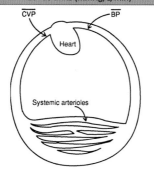

$\overline{CVP}$ $\overline{BP}$

Heart

Systemic arterioles

Example —

$$SVR = \frac{93 \text{ mmHg} - 5 \text{ mmHg}}{5 \text{ L/m}} \times 80$$

= 17.6 units (mmHg/L/min) x 80

= 1408 dynes•sec•cm^{-5}

80 = Correction factor for mmHg to dynes/cm^2
and L/m to cm^3/sec yielding dynes•sec•cm^{-5}

REGULATION OF SVR

Factors	Definition	Description / Notes
BLOOD VESSEL DIAMETER	Arteriole diameter is the primary determinant of SVR	SVR ≈ vessel diameter to 4th power 1/2 dia → 16 x ↑ SVR 1/4 dia → 256 x ↑ SVR
Local autoregulation	Vasomotor regulation of local arterioles in response to local metabolic demands	O_2 demand: ↓ demand → vasoconstriction ↑ demand → vasodilation Metabolites: ↑ metabolites → vasodilation ↓ metabolites → vasoconstriction (CO_2 lactic acid, H^+, bradykinins)
Autonomic nervous system	Sympathetic and parasympathetic stimulation of arterioles	
Baroreceptors	Pressure (stretch) receptors in aortic arch and carotid sinuses	Detect changes in BP Work by inhibiting vasomotor center ↑ BP → baroreceptors → ↓ vasomotor center → vasodilation → ↓ BP ↓ BP = opposite of above
Chemoreceptors	Chemical receptors in aortic and carotid bodies	Detect changes in O_2 and CO_2 (PaO_2 $PaCO_2$) which in turn influences the vasomotor center

Factors	Definition	Description / Notes
Hypothalamus	Regulates peripheral circulation in response to temperature	Stimulates or inhibits vasomotor center ↑ Temp → inhibition → vasodilation ↓ Temp → stimulation → vasoconstriction
Cerebral cortex	Regulates peripheral circulation in response to stress	Ex. pain, blushing, emotionally induced syncope
Humoral control	Circulating catecholamines	Released from adrenal medulla or nerve endings Effects are similar to sympathetic stimulation
Vessel elasticity	Vessel distensibility	↓ elasticity → ↑ SVR (Ex. arteriosclerosis, aortic stenosis)
BLOOD VOLUME	Absolute or relative volume	Blood volume changes must be significant before affecting SVR ↑ blood volume → little change in SVR due to venous capacitance (dilation) ↓ blood volume → little change in SVR due to vasoconstriction
BLOOD VISCOSITY	"Thickness" of fluid	↑ Viscosity = ↑ resistance to flow → ↑ SVR Viscosity ≈ hematocrit Clinically — usually of minor importance

Physiology

2-41

Factors	Definition	Description / Notes
KIDNEYS	Renin-angiotensin mechanism	↓ BP or flow to kidneys → ↑ renin → ↑ angiotensin I → ↑ angiotensin II angiotensin II → adrenal cortex → ↑ aldosterone → ↑ Na + H_2O retention → ↑ blood volume → ↑ BP angiotensin II → arteriole vasoconstriction → ↑ SVR → ↑ BP ↑ BP → opposite reactions

CAUSES OF CHANGES IN SVR

↑ SVR (↑ LV afterload)	↓ SVR (↓ LV afterload)
Generalized vasoconstriction:	Generalized vasodilation:
Decreased CO	Vasodilator therapy
Excessive catecholamine	Shock —
secretion	Anaphylactic
Hypertension	Hyperdynamic sepsis
Hypothermia	Neurogenic
Hypovolemia	
Stress response	Other:
Vasopressors	Anemia
	Aortic regurgitation
Decreased distensibility of	Cirrhosis
vessels:	
Aortic stenosis	
Arteriosclerosis	
Atherosclerosis	
Coarctation of aorta	

Effects of change in SVR

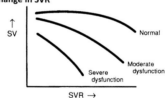

NOTE:

Normal heart —	SV normally remains constant with fluctuation in SVR
	$M\dot{v}O_2$ is directly related to SVR:

$$\uparrow SVR \rightarrow \uparrow M\dot{v}O_2$$
$$\downarrow SVR \rightarrow \downarrow M\dot{v}O_2$$

Myocardial dysfunction —	SV is inversely related to SVR
	$M\dot{v}O_2$ is directly related to SVR

$$\uparrow SVR \rightarrow \downarrow SV + \uparrow M\dot{v}O_2$$
$$\downarrow SVR \rightarrow \uparrow SV + \downarrow M\dot{v}O_2$$

CLINICAL NOTE

SVR is an indicator of LV afterload (LV afterload = BP dia + SVR)

PULMONARY VASCULAR RESISTANCE (PVR)

Definitions:

> Force the RV must overcome to maintain pulmonary blood flow
> Pulmonary blood vessel resistance to blood flow

Value:

$$PVR = \frac{PAMP - PAWP}{CO} \times 80$$

Normal PVR = 20 – 200 dynes•sec•cm^{-5}
= 0.25 – 2.5 units (mmHg/L/min)
≈ 1/6 SVR

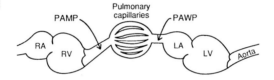

CLINICAL NOTE

PVR ≈ PADP - PAWP gradient (see Pg. 7-18,21).

Example:

PVR = $\frac{15 \text{ mmHg} - 8 \text{ mmHg}}{5 \text{ L/m}} \times 80$

= 1.4 units (mmHg/L/min) x 80

= 112 dynes•sec•cm^{-5}

80 = Correction factor for mmHg to dynes/cm^2 and L/m to cm^3/sec yielding dynes•sec•cm^{-5}

REGULATION OF PVR

Factors	Notes	Example
1. Autonomic Nervous System	Sympathetic dominates causing slight ↑ PVR	Primary pulmonary hypertension
2. Oxygen	↓ O_2 is a potent vasoconstrictor (opposite of systemic vessels)	Hypoxemia
3. Volume status	↑ volume → ↑ PVR	Pulmonary edema
4. pH	↓ pH → vasoconstriction	Acidemia
5. Cross-sectional area of pulmonary circulation	> 30% decrease → ↑ PVR	Pulmonary emboli Pulmonary stenosis
6. Drugs	Pulmonary vasoconstrictors (↑PVR) Pulmonary vasodilators (↓PVR)	Beraprost Bosentan Epinephrine Epoprosternol (Prostacyclin) Iloprost Norepinephrine Metaraminol Diltiazem Nifedipine Nitroprusside Nitrous oxide Sildenafil (Viagra) Treprostinal

Physiology

Note:

PVR ≈ 1/6 SVR

Flow can increase 3-4x before any ↑ PVR

↑ PVR → ↑ PAS + ↑ PAD + ↑ PAMP

Effects of change in PVR

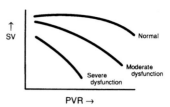

NOTE:

Normal heart —   SV normally remains constant with fluctuation in PVR

$M\dot{V}O_2$ is directly related to PVR:

$$\uparrow PVR \rightarrow \uparrow M\dot{V}O_2$$
$$\downarrow PVR \rightarrow \downarrow M\dot{V}O_2$$

Myocardial dysfunction — SV is inversely related to PVR
$M\dot{V}O_2$ is directly related to PVR

$$\uparrow PVR \rightarrow \downarrow SV + \uparrow M\dot{V}O_2$$
$$\downarrow PVR \rightarrow \uparrow SV + \downarrow M\dot{V}O_2$$

CLINICAL NOTE

PVR is an indicator of RV afterload (RV afterload = PADP + PVR)

3 Oxygen Monitoring

Oxygen Monitoring

OXYGEN MONITORING: SaO$_2$ AND S$\bar{\text{V}}$O$_2$

Overview

SaO$_2$ (and/or ABG's):	pulmonary system and oxygenation
	+
Hemodynamic monitoring:	cardiovascular system and perfusion
	——————————————
S$\bar{\text{V}}$O$_2$:	cardiopulmonary system meeting the tissues oxygen needs

O$_2$ supply -	O$_2$ demand =	O$_2$ reserve
SaO$_2$ -	$\dot{\text{V}}$O =	S$\bar{\text{V}}$O$_2$

Definition —	Intermittent or continuous monitoring of saturation of arterial blood by reflection of a light source off red blood cells.
Indication —	Conditions which may lead to rapidly changing O_2 saturations
Purpose —	Early and immediate detection of change in SaO_2, i.e.: 1. Warnings of hypoxemia 2. Assessment of ventilatory support 3. Assessment of other therapies
Techniques —	***Noninvasive Pulse Oximetry (SpO_2)*** Passing the light source through an ear, nose bridge, finger or toe ① (also measures pulse rate) *Invasive (SaO_2)* Light source is inserted into an artery via catheter
Procedure —	refer to operator's manual
Interpretation —	Normal SpO_2 and SaO_2 > 95% Normal acceptable clinical range 90-100%

Caution — SpO_2 measures oxyhemoglobin plus carboxy and methemoglobins. Hence, SpO_2 may be a poor indicator of SaO_2 even in the presence of small amounts of dysfunctional hemoglobins.

SpO_2 values may differ between various models of oximeters; do not interchange oximeters on the same patient.

Ensuring good waveform when available, and correlating SpO2 HR with HR monitored by other means improves validity of SpO2 reading.

> **Note:**
> Acceptable lower limit is usually per physician order. Any O_2 saturation below this lower limit demands immediate patient assessment.
>
> Trends are more important than absolute values. Baseline correlations should be made with PaO_2 &/or SaO_2 (Co-oximetry).

Oxygen Monitoring

Advantages

Direct, continuous SaO_2

Decreases need for frequent
ABG sticks

Continuous monitoring
of clinical trends,
procedures and therapies

Rapid response time
Infrequent sampling errors
Infrequent repositioning
required

Disadvantages

Clot formation (invasive)

Infection (invasive)

Won't detect hyperoxia

Accuracy affected by:
jaundice, patient
movement, skin
thickness, regional
blood flow, shock,
carboxyhemoglobin, etc.
(see next page)

Gives a late response to
ventilatory failure

① Sensors should be placed on an extremity where blood flow is
not diminished by either an arterial line or BP cuff.

Troubleshooting the Pulse Oximeter (SpO$_2$)

Problem	Possible Cause	Recommended Action
? Inaccurate SaO$_2$	Excessive patient movement	Quiet patient, if possible. Check security of sensor; replace if necessary. Move sensor to different site. Change type of sensor used. Use ECG signal synchronization. Select a longer (10-15 sec) averaging time, if possible.
	High carboxyhemoglobin or methemoglobin levels	Measure dysfunctional hemoglobin levels. Measure arterial blood gas.
	Reduced arterial blood flow	Do not place sensor on same side as indwelling arterial catheter or blood pressure cuff.
	Electrocautery interference	Move sensor as far as possible from cautery cable; change sites if necessary. Check sensor; replace if damp. Place oximeter plug into a different circuit from cautery unit.
	Excessive ambient light (surgical lamps, heating lamps, bilirubin lights, bright fluorescent lights, direct sunlight, dark fingernail polish, dark pigmented skin)	Cover sensor with opaque material.

Oxygen Monitoring

Problem	Possible Cause	Recommended Action
Loss of pulse signal	Constriction by sensor	Check sensor; move to a different site or change type of sensor used.
	Reduced arterial blood flow	Same as above.
	Excessive ambient light	Same as above.
	Anemia	Check patient's hemoglobin.
	Hypothermia	Warm monitoring site and replace sensor.
	Shock (hypotension, vaso-constriction)	Check patient's condition including vital signs.
Inaccurate pulse rate	Excessive patient motion	Same as above.
	Pronounced dicrotic notch on arterial waveform	Move sensor to a different site.
	Poor quality ECG signal	Check ECG leads; replace if necessary.
	Electrocautery interference	Same as above.

Reprinted with permission from Daily, E.K. and Schroeder, J.S.: *Techniques in Bedside Hemodynamic Monitoring,* 4th Ed. Copyright 1989 by C.V. Mosby Co., St. Louis.

Oxygen Monitoring

Definition — Intermittent or continuous monitoring of saturation of mixed venous blood.[1]

$$S\bar{v}O_2 = \text{reserve } O_2 \text{ supply:}$$
= a measure of the amount of O_2 left over and not used by the body tissues.

CLINICAL NOTE

$S\bar{v}O_2$ = indicates whether O_2 supply ($\dot{D}O_2$) is meeting O_2 demand ($\dot{V}O_2$).

O₂ supply	—	O₂ demand (consumption)	=	O₂ reserve
$\dot{D}O_2$	—	$\dot{V}O_2$	=	Venous O_2 supply
$CaO_2 \times CO$	—	$Ca\text{-}\bar{v}O_2 \times CO$	=	$C\bar{v}O_2 \times CO$
Simplified				
CaO_2	—	$Ca\text{-}\bar{v}O_2$	=	$C\bar{v}O_2$
Reflected by				
SaO_2	—	$Sa\text{-}\bar{v}O_2$	=	$S\bar{v}O_2$

$$S\bar{v}O_2 = 1 - \frac{Sa\text{-}\bar{v}O_2}{SaO_2}$$

If $SaO_2 = 1$, then

$$S\bar{v}O_2 = 1 - \frac{Ca\text{-}\bar{v}O_2}{CaO_2}$$

$$S\bar{v}O_2 = 1 - \frac{\dot{V}O_2}{\dot{D}O_2}$$

$$S\bar{v}O_2 = 1 - O_2 \text{ ER} \quad \text{(See also page 2-7)}$$

Caution — There is often little to no correlation between $S\bar{v}O_2$ and SaO_2, PaO_2, CO or Hgb, esp. in critically ill patients. The only consistent clinical correlation is the one between $S\bar{v}O_2$ and O_2 ER.

Therefore, $S\bar{v}O_2$ reflects the amount of O_2 consumed (demand) by the body tissues.

---

[1]—See next page.

Oxygen Monitoring

Indications — Conditions of rapidly changing or unstable cardiopulmonary function.

Purpose —
1. Early and immediate detection of hemodynamic changes

    Provides "real time" information and data for calculating several hemodynamic equations. $S\bar{v}O_2$ changes often precede significant changes in hemodynamics.

2. Early and immediate detection of a threatened O_2 delivery system

    Sensitive indicator of O_2 supply/demand balance

3. Assess effectiveness of therapeutic and ventilatory interventions

Techniques & Procedures

Intermittent sampling — blood gas sample from the distal port of a PA catheter. (See Pg. 7-14)

Continuous monitoring — a fiberoptic catheter is within a PA catheter and an oximeter. (See Pg. 7-15)

① $S\bar{v}O_2$: Venous blood is considered mixed after it has circulated through the right side of the heart and entered the pulmonary artery.

SvO_2: Saturation of venous blood returning from a particular region of the body (before mixing). It is reflective of the O_2 supply/demand balance of the area served (eg., normal heart $SvO_2 = 30\%$. Normal kidney $SvO_2 = 90\%$). This value is rarely used clinically.

SvO₂ Interpretation

Normal $S\bar{v}O_2$ = 75%	(Normal $P\bar{v}O_2$ = 40)
Normal $S\bar{v}O_2$ range = 60-80%	(Normal $P\bar{v}O_2$ range = 35-42)

Interpreting changes ①

> ↓ $S\bar{v}O_2$ ≤ 5% = maybe clinically insignificant
>
> ↓ $S\bar{v}O_2$ ≥ 10% for ≥ 3 min = impending deterioration ②

$S\bar{v}O_2$ > 80%　　supply > demand　⎫　O_2 reserve is not

$S\bar{v}O_2$ 60-80%　　supply = demand　⎬　being used

$S\bar{v}O_2$ < 60%　　supply < demand　⎫　O_2 reserve is
　　　　　　　　　　　　　　　　　⎬　being used
　　　　　　　　　　　　　　　　　⎭　(↓ supply or
　　　　　　　　　　　　　　　　　　　↑ demand)

$S\bar{v}O_2$ < 50%
　　point at which anaerobic　⎫　O_2 reserve
　　metabolism (and lactic　　⎬　used up
　　acidosis) begins
　　(Reflects $PvO_2 \approx 28$)

$S\bar{v}O_2$ < 30%
　　indicates insufficient tissue　⎫　O_2 reserve
　　O_2, clinical coma　　　　　⎬　used up
　　occurs (reflects $PvO_2 \approx 20$)

①　$S\bar{v}O_2$ monitoring decreases the need for routine ABG's and allows for minimal CO determinations (only when hemodynamically indicated). *Same values in children.*

　　Caution —　A normal $S\bar{v}O_2$ does not always mean a normal or stable CV status (see Pg 3-14).

②　An immediate evaluation of the patient's O_2 supply/demand status, catheter position and/or calibration is indicated. (The 3 minute time may be extended to 10 minutes after a positional Δ.)

Alterations in SvO₂

Alteration	Physiological Causes	Pathological Causes (examples)	Physiological Compensation ①	Therapeutic Compensation
↓ SvO₂ (< 60%)	↓ arterial O₂ supply:		↑ arterial O₂ supply:	
	↓ CO ② ↓ HR	arrhythmias	↑ CO ③ ↑ HR	CO therapy ④ – volume or drugs ↑ HR
	↓ SV	hypovolemic shock acute MI CHF	↑ SV ↑ preload ↓ afterload ↑ contractility	↑ SV ↑ preload ↑ afterload ↑ contractility
	↓CaO₂ ↓ SaO₂, ⑤ ↓ PaO₂	hypoxemia	↑ CaO₂ ↑ SaO₂ ↑ PaO₂ ⑥ ↑ VA ↑ RR ↑ VT Improve V/Q	O₂ therapy Ventilator therapy (CPAP, PEEP)
	↓ Hgb ⑦	anemia hemorrhage	↑ Hgb production (chronic only)	Optimize fluid status Blood or blood products
			↓ Venous O₂ reserve ⑧ ↓ CⱽO₂ ↓ SⱽO₂ ↓ PⱽO₂	

3-11

Alteration	Physiological Causes	Pathological Causes (examples)	Physiological Compensation ①	Therapeutic Compensation
↑ Tissue demand (↑ O₂ consumption):	↑ muscle work: ↑ WOB ambulation bathing burns seizures shivering weighing ↑ anxiety: agitation pain suctioning CPT ↑ body temp	Pulmonary disease dyspnea surgery (resp. therapist and/or nurse) fever sepsis thyroid storm	↑ arterial O₂ supply (as above) ↓ venous O₂ reserve (as above)	↓ muscle work: ↓ WOB - (CPAP, PPV) ↓ patient manipulation ↓ anxiety: minimize suctioning and stress drug therapy ↓ body temp: antibiotic therapy
↓ arterial O₂ supply: and ↑ tissue demand (any combination of the above) R-L shunt		Eg: COPD (↓ SaO₂) + MI (↓ CO) COPD (acute exacerbation) (↓ SaO₂, ↑ WOB, sepsis, fever) CHF (↓ CO) + pulmonary edema (↓ SaO₂) Chest trauma (↓ SaO₂, ↓ CO, ↓ Hgb, ↑ WOB, pain)		
			Variable	Correct shunt

3-12

Oxygen Monitoring

Alteration	Physiological Causes	Pathological Causes (examples)	Physiological Compensation ①	Therapeutic Compensation
↑ SvO_2 (> 80%)	↑ arterial O_2 supply: ↑ CO anxiety excitement	septic shock iatrogenic (CO therapy)	variable	eliminate cause adjust CO therapy
	↑ CaO_2 ↓ tissue demand (↓ O_2 consumption):	excessive O_2 therapy anesthesia cyanide poison, coma endotoxins ethanol intoxication induced muscle paralysis hypothermia Left shift of oxyhemoglobin curve: ↑ pH ↓ 2, 3DPG septicemia	variable variable	adjust O_2 therapy eliminate cause

3-13

Alteration	Physiological Causes	Pathological Causes (examples)	Physiological Compensation [1]	Therapeutic Compensation
Normal $S\bar{v}O_2$ (60-80%)	L-R shunt:	Cardiac or pulmonary shunts	variable	correct shunt
	Caution — A "normal" $S\bar{v}O_2$ may be a combination of $\downarrow S\bar{v}O_2$ from one cause and a corresponding $\uparrow S\bar{v}O_2$ from another cause (eg: acute MI with septicemia)			

Footnotes [1] - [8]: See next page.

① **Physiological Compensation of $\downarrow$ S$\bar{v}$O$_2$**

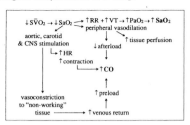

Note: Compensation is often severely impaired in critically ill patients.

② $\downarrow$ CO is the most common cause of $\downarrow$ S$\bar{v}$O$_2$.

③ $\uparrow$ CO is the body's primary compensatory mechanism.

A healthy adult heart may increase CO 3-5 × normal (15-25 L/m). A compromised heart may not be able to compensate at all.

④ S$\bar{v}$O$_2$ is a sensitive indicator of how well CO therapy is working (the appropriateness and effectiveness of preload, afterload and/or contractility manipulations).

⑤ A transient $\downarrow$ SvO$_2$ may be a reflection of a rapid and transient $\downarrow$ SaO$_2$ in which the CO cannot compensate fast enough (eg., ET suctioning).

⑥ This compensatory mechanism is limited, especially if the pulmonary system is compromised.

⑦ A gradual decrease in S$\bar{v}$O$_2$ may be a reflection of a gradual loss of blood (ie: internal bleeding).

⑧ The venous O$_2$ supply (reserve) is a major source of "extra" O$_2$ when the supply < demand. This reserve, however, is a "secondary" supply and is tapped only after every attempt is first made to increase the arterial O$_2$ supply.

The $\uparrow$ O$_2$ extraction from the blood occurs by simple diffusion.

O$_2$ extraction can increase approximately 3x until S$\bar{v}$O$_2$ $\downarrow$ to 30% (P$\bar{v}$O$_2$ 20).

Venous O$_2$ reserve can only last 3-4 minutes before depleted if the arterial O$_2$ supply stops completely (ie: cardiac arrest).

Example of maximal physiological compensation for ↓ S$\bar{v}$O$_2$:

$$\boxed{\dot{V}O_2 = Ca - \bar{v}O_2 \times CO} \quad \text{(see Pg 2-7)}$$

$$= (CaO_2 - C\bar{v}O_2) \times CO \times 10$$

$$= [(SaO_2 \times Hgb \times 1.36) + (PaO_2 \times 0.0031)] -$$
$$\quad [(S\bar{v}O_2 \times Hgb \times 1.36) + (P\bar{v}O_2 \times 0.0031)] \times CO \times 10$$

$$= [(1.0 \times 15 \text{ gm} \times 1.36) + (100 \times 0.0031)] -$$
$$\quad [(0.30 \times 15 \text{ gm} \times 1.36) + (20 \times 0.0031)] \times 15 \text{ L/m}① \times 10$$

$$= [(1.0 - 0.3)② (15 \text{ gm} \times 1.36) + (100 - 20)③$$
$$\quad (0.0031)] \times 15 \text{ L/m} \times 10$$

$$= 2180 \text{ mL/min}$$

$$2180 \text{ mL/min} = 9 \times \text{normal of } 250 \text{ mL/min}$$

①	↑ CO 3x	(5 L/m → 15 L/m)
②	↑ O$_2$ ER 3x	(0.25 → 0.70)
		9x

② SaO$_2$ − S$\bar{v}$O$_2$ ≈ O$_2$ ER (see Pg. 2-7)

③ PaO$_2$ − P$\bar{v}$O$_2$ = a − vDO$_2$ (see Pg. 1-9)

Troubleshooting the S$\bar{v}$O$_2$ monitor (see manufacturer's guidelines).

4 Blood Sampling

BLOOD SAMPLING

Blood samples may be obtained from any invasive line.

> (Drawing from an LA line is not advisable due to potential embolization.)

Line	Type of Blood		
	Arterial	Venous	Mixed Venous
A- line	✔		
CVP		✔	
PA proximal		✔	
PA distal			✔

CLINICAL NOTE

1. Draw only the amount necessary.
2. Limit number of samples (try to arrange for all samples to be drawn at same time).
3. Line samples are not recommended for blood cultures

Procedures:

A-line	—	See Pg. 5-19
CVP line	—	See Pg. 6-11
PA line	—	See Pg. 7-14

5 Blood Pressure Monitoring

Blood Pressure

Arterial Pressure Monitoring

Overview of Technique

Indirect

Palpation (pg 5-4)
Auscultation (pg 5-7)
Automatic monitoring (pg 5-8)
Doppler Ultrasound (pg 5-8)

Direct

Monitored occlusion technique (pg 5-8)
Intra-arterial catheter (A-line) (pg 5-9)

INDIRECT

Palpation of Arterial Pressure (Pulse) [1]

Parameter	Clinical Note
Rate	Normal = 60-100 bpm (< 60 = bradycardia, > 100 = tachycardia)
	Note: appropriateness and hemodynamic consequence of HR is more clinically significant than an absolute value
	Palpation rate may vary from actual HR. Best way to count: listen at PMI with a stethoscope (or watch EKG monitor) while palpating the peripheral pulse and compare number of heartbeats with number of perfusing beats.
Rhythm	Note if rhythm is regular. Note any irregularity.

[1] During initial exam, check presence and character of all major pulses (carotid, radial, brachial, femoral, popliteal, post-tibial and dorsalis pedis).
Periodic assessment of each pulse is essential, especially following catheterization.

Parameter

Volume

Clinical Note

Pulse volume = strength of pulse = LVSV

Note: Carotid and brachial vessels are more reliable in assessing LVSV than the distal radial and pedal vessels.

Rule of thumb
If can palpate:	then BP ≥:
Radial	80
Femoral	70
Carotid	60

Amplitude
4 = bounding
3 = full, increased
2 = normal
1 = diminished
0 = absent

↑ Pulse volume (↑ LVSV)
Hyperdynamic states (↑ CO)
Anemia
Early sepsis
Emotion (anxiety)
Exercise
Fever
Hyperthroidism

↓ Pulse volume (↓ LVSV)
Hypodynamic states (↓ CO)
Hypovolemia
LV dysfunction
Tacharrhythmias
Vessel abnormalities
Atherosclerosis
Dissecting aortic aneurysm

Note: Sudden disappearance of a pulse is indicative of a systemic embolus. It is frequently accompanied by pallor of extremity, pain and temperature change in the extremity.

5-5

Blood Pressure

Parameter	Clinical Note
Equality of volume	Check equality of strength with each beat. (See also 5-21)
	Pulsus alternans:
	Causes: Regular alternation of weak and strong pulses. Normal heart with severe tachycardia, LHF with hypertension or aortic stenosis, failure due to cardiomyopathies.
	Pulsus paradoxicus: ↓ pulse volume during inspiration ↑ pulse volume during expiration (difference ≥ 10 mmHg)
	Usually a difference of ≥ 20 mmHg is needed to feel the difference.
	Causes: Cardiac tamponade (pulse may disappear during inspiration). Constrictive pericarditis Hypovolemic shock Pulmonary embolus Severe COPD (asthma)
Pressure: BP sys	Procedure: Place arm at level of heart, place BP cuff around upper arm, palpate brachial or radial pulse, inflate cuff 20-30 mmHg above point at which pulse is lost, deflate cuff slowly. BP sys = pressure at which pulse returns.
	Advantage — "Quick" check of BP sys Disadvantage — highly subjective, limited value

Technique —

Place arm at level of heart, place BP cuff around upper arm, place stethoscope over brachial artery. Inflate cuff to 20-30 mmHg above suspected BP sys. Deflate cuff slowly ($\leq$ 3 mmHg/sec).

BP sys = appearance of sounds.

BP dia = change in character or intensity of sounds or cessation of sounds.

> **Note:** Some clinicians and AHA recommend recording 3 levels:
> BP sys / BP dia / cessation of sounds

When 2 points are recorded:	When 3 points are recorded:
BP sys = appearance	BP sys = appearance
BP dia (2) = cessation	BP dia (1) = change
	BP dia (2) = cessation

(BP dia (1) is considered to be the closest approximation to true diastolic pressure)

Measurements should be taken with arm at heart level.
Pulse sounds are best heard with the bell of the stethoscope.
Baseline measurements should be made in both arms.
(> 15 mmHg difference may indicate an obstructive lesion in aorta or subclavian arteries.)

Errors and Abnormal Findings Common to the Auscultatory Technique

Error/Finding	Cause
False high BP reading	BP cuff too small or loose or arm location below heart.
False low BP reading	BP cuff too large, obese patient, or arm location higher than heart.
False low BP sys False high BP dia	Rapid cuff deflation
Auscultatory gap: BP sys appears, disappears, then reappears	Hypertension

(continued on next page)

Error/Finding	Cause
Paradoxical BP: Systolic gradient > 10 mmHg①	Significant pulmonary or cardiac compromise (esp. cardiac tamponade)

① Systolic gradient =

BP sys during E (sounds only during E)	minus −	BP sys during I + E (sounds during both I + E)

CLINICAL NOTE

Indirect methods become inaccurate at extreme pressures (very low or very high)

Automatic Monitoring

A device which automatically and periodically performs the auscultatory technique.

Doppler Ultrasound

A transceiver is placed over an artery, emits and receives high frequency signals, and calculates arterial wall movement (BP).

Indication:	To obtain accurate systolic arterial pressure.
Procedure:	Apply cuff.
	Add gel to probe.
	Place probe on artery below cuff.
	Turn on Doppler.
	Listen for pulsatile hissing sound.
	Inflate cuff rapidly until hiss stops.
	Lower pressure slowly until hiss reappears (systolic pressure).
	Record pressure and which extremity was used.

DIRECT

Monitored Occlusion Technique

Equipment:	Indwelling A-line plus sphygmomanometer
Technique:	apply BP cuff to arm with A-line
	Inflate cuff until waveform on monitor disappears
	Deflate slowly
	Observe when waveform reappears (1st blip on monitor), note BP sys on monitor, and simultaneously note BP sys on cuff manometer.

CLINICAL NOTE

This technique is used primarily to check for proper functioning of the electronics. Check system electronics if values vary significantly.

A-LINE PRESSURE MONITORING

Definition: Monitoring of hemodynamic parameters via an intra-arterial catheter.

Indications:

1. BP monitoring
   Conditions of instability
   Assessment of therapeutic interventions
2. ABG sampling

> **Note:** A-lines are not indicated for medication administration or fluid maintenance.

Insertion Sites:

Factors to Consider	AXILLARY ①	BRACHIAL	RADIAL ②	FEMORAL ③	DORSALIS PEDIS ④
Large size	X	X		X	
Good accessibility	X	X	X	X	X
Good collateral circulation	X		X		X
Low injury risk at insertion			X		X
Close to heart ⑤	X	X			
Good patient comfort / mobility			X		
Easy to control and/or observe bleeding			X		X

① Insertion is technically difficult.
② Most commonly preferred site, contraindicated if no or poor collateral circulation.
③ Many clinicians like femoral insertions despite the disadvantages.
④ Not preferred for BP monitoring due to distance from heart and regional blood flow variations. Not recommended if patient ambulatory or has peripheral vascular disease.
⑤ Vessels far from heart (except femoral) may not reflect central aortic pressure in shock states or peripheral vasoconstriction.

Blood Pressure

EQUIPMENT: COMPONENTS

Item	Purpose
Amplifier	An electrical device which amplifies and conditions the small electrical signal from the transducer (usually a part of the pressure monitor).
Automatic (continuous) flush device	A device which insures a solution flow of 3-5 cc/hr. to prevent clotting and backflow. Also used for rapid manual flushing and dynamic response testing.
Catheter	Intra-arterial (or CVP or PA).
Fluid reservoir and Pressure bag	A bag of heparinized normal saline (flush solution) surrounded by a pressure cuff pumped to 300 mmHg to counter the BP resistance.
IV tubing, connectors and stopcocks	A rigid pressure tubing system which connects the transducer and reservoir to the invasive catheter.
Manifold	Holding device for transducer (usually onto an IV pole). Adjustable for leveling transducer to appropriate level.
Pressure Monitor	A display device for pressure magnitude and/or waveform by oscilloscope, digital readout or permanent recording device.
Transducer	A device which converts mechanical energy (BP) into electrical energy (display readout).

Components of an A-Line

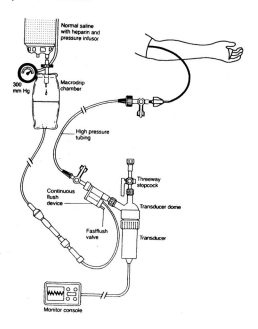

Adapted from Smith RN: Invasive pressure monitoring. *Am J Nurs* 1978: 9:1514-1521.

EQUIPMENT: Assembly

Note: The following is a general guideline. Employ hospital and manufacturer's protocols whenever possible.

1. Switch on pressure monitor to warm up.
2. Always use aseptic technique.
3. Prepare flush solution: Add 1-4 units heparin/cc of solution to the saline IV bag and label (except patients with heparin sensitivity).
4. Connect tubing to IV bag and flush. (Remove all air from IV bag.)
5. Place pressure bag around IV bag (do not pump up yet).
6. Set up transducer and connect to manifold (or patient's wrist).
7. Connect IV bag to proximal end of flush device.
8. Connect flush device to stopcock on transducer dome.
9. Connect tubing to distal end of flush device.
10. Flush entire system, clearing all bubbles (use the stopcock with syringe not attached to flush device). (Follow manufacturer's directions.)
11. Pressurize bag to 300 mmHg.
12. Connect tubing from distal end of flush device to patient catheter (after insertion). Insure no air bubbles.
13. Insure drip rate of 1-5 ml/hr; 3-6 minidrops/min
14. Connect transducer to pressure monitor.
15. Zero and calibrate (see next page).
16. Secure with tape all non-Luer lock connections.
17. Label and date all tubings.

EQUIPMENT: Zeroing and Calibration

Note: General guidelines only. Follow manufacturer's suggested procedure.

Note: Patient should be supine or as close as possible to supine. First, place transducer at appropriate level in relation to patient:

A-line—place at level of catheter tip in the cannulated artery. (To get an accurate reading of aortic root pressure and CPP, place both the transducer and catheter tip (ie: extremity) at level of right atrium, phlebostatic axis, see CVP, Pg. 6-16.)

CVP catheter ⎰ Place at level of phlebostatic axis (right atrium).
PA catheter ⎱ See CVP, Pg. 6-16.

Zeroing — Balancing the transducer to atmospheric pressure (zero).

    Procedure:
1. Insure monitoring system is warmed up.
2. Insure no air bubbles in tubing system.
3. Turn stopcock on transducer dome (connected to flush device) off to patient and open to air.
4. Adjust "zero" to read zero on display.
5. Adjust "cal" to appropriate readout (eg. 200).
6. Check for return to zero.
7. Close dome stopcock to air and open to patient.
8. Zero once each shift. or when values are in question.

Calibration — Balancing the transducer to a known pressure using a mercury manometer is no longer recommended because of the risk of air embolism to the patient.

A-Line Insertion Technique

Percutaneous Insertion Procedure

1. Explain procedure to patient
2. Prepare monitoring equipment (see Pg. 5-12)
3. Use aseptic technique.
4. Insure collateral circulation (see next page)
5. Palpate artery to insure exact location
6. Prepare insertion site
7. Insert needle and catheter into artery (Various techniques are used)
8. Attach heparinized flush line and gently flush
9. Apply firm pressure to puncture site for 5-10 min.
10. Secure catheter in place and tighten all connections
11. Apply antimicrobial ointment and dry sterile dressing
12. Monitor pressure and waveform for proper tip positioning
13. Check adequacy of distal blood flow (see next page)
14. Observe for complications (see Pgs. 5-28 and 5-31).

Surgical Cutdown

Performed if percutaneous puncture is unsuccessful or technically difficult (beyond the scope of this book).

Blood Pressure

Checking for collateral circulation

Radial artery (Allen's test) —

1. Reduce blood in hand.
   a. Have patient clench and unclench hand several times or
   b. Raise hand over head for several seconds (modified Allen's test).
2. Compress both radial and ulnar arteries.
3. Have patient unclench hand (or lower arm).
4. Release pressure over ulnar artery.
5. Observe color return to hand.

   Color return in:
≤ 7 sec	=	good circulation.
7-15 sec	=	impaired circulation.
> 15 sec	=	inadequate circulation.

6. Use of radial artery is contraindicated if color does not return in 7 seconds.

Dorsalis pedis artery —

1. Occlude dorsalis pedis and posterior tibial arteries with one hand.
2. Blanch nail bed of big toe with other hand for 15 seconds.
3. Release big toe and posterior tibial artery.
4. Watch for color return (same as Allen's test).

Note: Optional methods include Doppler flow probe and finger-pulse transducer.

Blood Pressure

Maintenance of A-Line

Post-insertion protocol — (General guideline only, employ hospital protocol whenever possible.)

Check all connections and keep all connections and puncture site visible

Immobilize extremity (positional changes may ↑ or ↓ patency).

Label all lines and date.

Insure continuous flow of 2-5 mL/hr of heparinized IV solution. (Caution for thrombocytopenia or other coagulopathies.)

Continuously monitor pressure tracings.

Cover insertion site with antiseptic ointment.

Insure disconnect alarm for monitoring system.

Keep pressure bag inflated at 300 mmHg.

(As bag pressure decreases, infusion decreases.)

Every hr —

Monitor UO.

Every 2 hr —

Check distal pulses (use Doppler if necessary).

> **Note:** If pulse is absent, remove catheter and restore circulation with thrombolytic therapy or embolectomy, if necessary.

Check circulation (color, capillary refill, temp), sensation (tingling, pain, numbness) and movement of extremity.

Check insertion site for bleeding or infection.

> **Note:** If bleeding occurs, apply firm pressure above site for 5-10 minutes. A thrombosis may occur following manual pressure.

Perform bedside check of integrity of catheter and tubing system:

Technique 1 —

Occlude artery with finger, proximal to indwelling catheter.

Observe waveform:

Rapid downward movement.

Remove finger quickly.

A rapid return to baseline indicates an open system.

A slow return suggests partial occlusion of tubing or catheter.

Technique 2 —

Activate fast flush for 1-2 seconds.

Observe waveform:

Rapid upwards, then rapid downwards to below baseline, then back to baseline.

A quick return represents a "clean flush" and open system.

A slow return suggests partial occlusion of tubing or catheter.

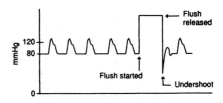

CLINICAL NOTE

Always aspirate and discard blood before flushing.

If blood return is not obtained, do not flush.

Flushing with a syringe should be gentle and small volume (2-5 mL).

Check all connections.

Document pressures and waveforms.

Every 8 hrs. or PRN

Evaluate CV, respiratory, renal and neurological status.

Zero balance monitoring system (see Pg. 5-12).

Replace all potentially contaminated equipment.

Infection Control

Insure aseptic technique at all times.

Change dressings q 24 hrs.

Change solutions, stopcocks, transducers, tubing, and manifold q 48 hrs.

Remove catheter ASAP or after 72-96 hrs. (↑ infection rate after 48 hrs.)

Cap all stopcocks not in use. (Keep caps sterile and closed as much as possible.)

All parts should be flushed until clear of blood.

Insure sterile infusates.

Protocol for dressing change (General guidelines only, employ hospital protocol):

Explain to patient.

Scrub hands with appropriate solution.

Don sterile gloves.

Remove dressing.

Observe site for infection, drainage, etc.

Remove gloves, scrub hands again.

Don second pair of sterile gloves.

Drape site with 4 × 4 sterile gauze.

Cleanse site with idophor solution.

Apply anti-microbial ointments and sterile dressing.

Apply tincture of benzoin to surrounding area.

Secure dressing with tape or label.

CLINICAL NOTE

Hands are main source of infection — insure proper and vigorous handwashing.

Keep number of line invasions to a minimal.

Keep number of personnel having line access to a minimum.

The plastic sleeve around catheter may give a false sense of security — microbial growth is frequently present.

Infection rates dramatically increase after 96 hours.

If infection is suspected, remove catheter and send tip to lab for culture and sensitivity.

Signs and Symptoms of Catheter-Related Sepsis

↑ body temp	Δ in CO	chills
↑ glucose	Δ in mental status	diaphoresis
↑ HR	Δ in WBC and platelets	malaise
↑ RR		

Blood Pressure

Signs and Symptoms of Site Infection

Redness at site	fever
Tenderness at site	chills
Purulent discharge	↑WBC
Pain at or above site	

Drawing a Blood Sample from an A-Line

1. Use aseptic technique.
2. Remove sterile cap from unused port of the most proximal of stopcocks to the insertion site. (Place cap in sterile gauze.)
3. Attach sterile syringe (3 mL).
4. Turn stopcock off to flush solution and on to patient.
5. Gently withdraw 3 mL of blood (to clear line of heparin solution and possible clots).
6. Turn stopcock off to all three ports.
7. Remove syringe and discard.
8. Place a second sterile syringe on stopcock (should be heparinized if for ABG analysis).

    To heparinize a syringe (many syringes are pre-heparinized):
    1. Use aseptic technique.
    2. Withdraw 0.5 ml of 1:1,000 Na heparin with a sterile syringe.
    3. Coat inside of syringe with heparin.
    4. Expel excess heparin.
9. Turn stopcock on to patient.
10. Withdraw desired amount of blood.
11. Turn stopcock off to sample port and on to patient.
12. Remove syringe (if for ABG analysis: remove air bubbles, cap, rotate to mix with heparin, label and place on ice).
13. Flush system for 1-3 seconds.
14. Turn stopcock off to patient and on to sample port.
15. Flush sample port (collect fluid with a sterile gauze).
16. Turn stopcock off to sample port and back on to patient.
17. Replace sterile cap.
18. Resume IV flow.

Note: Newer closed systems allow collection without opening to the air.

Blood Pressure

Arterial Pressures ② —

Parameter	Normal (Range)	Reflective of:
BP sys ③	120 mmHg (100-140 mmHg)	LV systolic pressure
BP dia ④	80 mmHg (60-80 mmHg)	Runoff and aortic elasticity
$\overline{BP}$ (MAP) ⑤	93 mmHg (70-95 mmHg)	CO × SVR
PP ⑥	40 mmHg (20-80 mmHg)	SV and arterial compliance

① Always use other clinical assessments in conjunction with hemodynamic parameters for accuracy.

② Accuracy depends on:
   Correct transducer positioning
   Proper patient positioning (patient should be in same position each time)
   Proper monitoring system zero and calibration

③ BP sys increases in distal vessels
   (femoral BP sys = 20-50 mmHg > brachial BP sys)

④ BP dia is same in distal vessels
   BP dia is greatly affected by HR ($\uparrow$ HR $\rightarrow$ $\uparrow$ BP dia)
   BP dia greatly affects CPP (CPP = BP dia − PAWP)
   (Hence, HR greatly affects CPP)

⑤ $\overline{BP}$ is same in distal vessels
   $$\overline{BP} = \frac{BP\ sys + 2\ BP\ dia}{3}$$

⑥ PP = BP sys − BP dia

ARTERIAL PRESSURE VARIATIONS

Variation	Causes
↑ Arterial pressures	**Disease/Disorders** Aortic insufficiency (↑ BP sys, ↓ BP dia, ↑ PP) Arteriosclerosis Systemic hypertension **Drugs** Inotropes Vasopressors (↑ SVR)

↓ Arterial pressures	Arrhythmias
	  a-fib (highly variable)
	  PVC's (↓ SV → ↓ BP)
	SV decreased (↓ BP sys, ↓ PP,
	  normal contour)
	  LVF
	  Shock
	  Cardiac tamponade
	  etc.
	Obstruction to LV output
	  Aortic stenosis (↓ BP sys,
	  ↓ PP, damped contour)
	  Mitral stenosis
	
	Vasodilators (↓ SVR)

AORTIC INSUFFICIENCY

150
100
20
0

Note: Insure proper transducer level and proper zero and calibration.

Blood Pressure

Blood Pressure

Variation	Causes

↑ Pulse pressure	<u>↑ SV</u>
	Aortic regurgitation
	Hypervolemia
	Some bradycardias
	
	<u>↑ Ejection velocity</u>
	Drugs - dobutamine
	          dopamine
	          isoproterenol
		<u>↑ Afterload (↑ SVR)</u>
		Arteriosclerosis
		Hypertension
		
		<u>↓ Afterload (↓ SVR)</u>
		Anemia
		Anxiety
		Exercise
		Fever
		Hyperthyroid

↓ Pulse pressure	<u>↓ SV</u> Heart failure Shock <u>↑ Ejection time</u> Aortic stenosis	<u>↑ Afterload (↑ SVR)</u> Increased norepinephrine Metabolic acidosis Severe cold Shock

Note:

Vessel Variations:

Coarctation of aorta— ↑ BP in head and upper extremities, ↓ BP (or norm BP) in lower

Stenosis— ↑ BP proximal to the stenosis, ↓ BP distal

Arterial Pressure Waveforms —

Significance — Reflect function and pressure changes in LV and SVR

Description — See also Pg. 2-22, overview of physiology

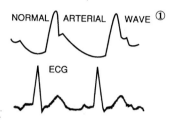

NORMAL ARTERIAL WAVE ①

ECG

Systole = Anacrotic limb plus first part of dicrotic limb down to dicrotic notch

Diastole = Dicrotic notch to next anacrotic limb

Shape and pressures change with anatomic site (↑ BP sys, waveform narrows, rises more sharply, ↓ dicrotic notch)

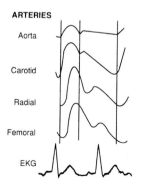

ARTERIES

Aorta

Carotid

Radial

Femoral

EKG

① *Waveform is the same in children.*

Blood Pressure

ARTERIAL PRESSURE WAVEFORM VARIATIONS

Variations		Description	Causes
Named variations: Pulsus alternans	120 — 100 —	Amplitude varies: Every other beat is larger	Alternating ventricular contractility: Arrhythmias LVF
Pulsus bisferiens	120 —	Two systolic peaks	Aortic regurgitation Hypertrophy cardiomyopathy Hyperthyroidism
Pulsus paradoxicus	120 — 100 —	↓ BP sys > 10 mmHg during spontaneous inspiration	Cardiac tamponade Constrictive pericarditis COPD Hypovolemic shock Pulmonary embolus Severe asthma
Reverse pulsus paradoxicus	140 — 120 —	↑ BP sys > 10 mmHg during positive pressure ventilation	Hypovolemia
Pulsus parvus	100 — 80	Weak pulse (↓ BP sys) with ↓ PP	↓CO: Aortic stenosis LVF Shock

Variations	Description		Causes
Pulsus bigeminus	BIGEMINAL PULSE	Amplitude and rhythm varies Every other beat weak and irregular and coupled with normal beats	Arrhythmias - esp. PVCs (Premature beats → ↓ SV)
Pulsus Corrigans	WATER-HAMMER PULSE	Strong or bounding with ↑ PP	↑SV: anemia aortic regurgitation essential hypertension PDA thyrotoxicosis
Specific feature variations;			
Fast upstroke	120 — 60 —	Quick ventricular ejection: Quick rise and sharp systolic point Also ↓BP dia and ↑PP	Cardiac disease: Mitral regurgitation Aortic regurgitation Systemic disease: Anemia Arteriosclerosis Thyrotoxicosis
Slow upstroke	120 —	Slow ventricular ejection: Slow rise	Aortic stenosis CHF with ↓ SV
↓ Dicrotic notch		Dicrotic notch ≤ 1/3 peak systolic pressure	↓ CO

Variations		Description	Causes
Pathologic conditions: Aortic regurgitation	120 —	Rapid upstroke ↑ BP sys → Dicrotic notch ↑PP	Aortic regurgitation
Aortic stenosis	120 —	Slow upstroke Usually ↓ BP sys → Dicrotic notch → PP	Aortic stenosis
Arrhythmias	120 — PAC 120 — PVC	Beat-to-beat variations: Small and early waveforms Varying sizes and intervals	Premature atrial contractions Premature junctional Premature ventricular contractions Atrial fibrillation Atrial tachyarrhythmias
Cardiac tamponade		↓ BP sys > 10 mmHg during spontaneous inspiration (See pulsus paradoxus, Pg. 10-9)	
Shock or severe hypotension	100 —	Small waveforms Slow upstroke → BP sys (< 90 mmHg)	

Variations	Description	Causes
Systemic hypertension	180 — 100 — Large waveforms, rapid upstroke, ↑ BP syst (> 140 mmHg) ↑ BP dial (> 90 mmHg)	
Mechanical causes: Damping	120 — Small rounded waveform Slow upstroke → Dicrotic notch → PP(↓ BP sys & ↑ BP dia)	Air bubbles in system Catheter lodged against vessel wall Partial clot (Note: very similar to waveform of aortic stenosis)
Inaccurate zero or calibrate	Variable	Electrical failure Infrequent or poor calibration Thermal changes in transducer Change in transducer reference level
Fling or whip	120 — Erratic or "noisy" with sharp negative or positive waves	Excessive catheter tip movement Excess tubing Rapid HR

5-27

Blood Pressure

A-LINE COMPLICATIONS TO WATCH FOR

Complication	Cause	Preventive Care / Treatment / Notes
Bleedback	Inadequate pressure on IV bag Loose connection	Insure pressure of 300 mmHg on bag. Note: if blood reaches transducer, the transducer should be replaced. Tighten (tape) loose connections. Use Luer-lock stopcocks.
	Loss of infusate Stopcock open to patient	Maintain IV solution Close stopcock
Hemorrhage	Loose connection	Tighten loose connection. Use Luer-locks. Insure all connecting sites are visible.
	Bleeding at puncture site	Watch for bruising, firmness or swelling. Apply manual pressure for 5-15 min. Restrict extremity movement. Remove catheter if necessary. Apply elastic tape or sandbag until bleeding stops.
Embolism		
Air	Air entry during insertion, tubing changes, blood samples, or giving meds.	Keep system free of air and keep connections tight. Remove any air that enters system. Keep patient flat when opening a subclavian system (CVP) and have patient hold breath at end expiration.

Complication	Cause	Preventive Care / Treatment / Notes
Thrombus	Blood clot from catheter tip	Insure steady flow of heparinized infusate. Always aspirate (1-2 ml) first, before flushing. **Note:** If aspiration fails to produce a blood return — do not flush. Remove catheter.
	Catheter kink Poor fluid flow Vessel trauma	Avoid vigorous flushing. Increased risk in patients with hypercoaguable states: cancer, fever, MI, polycythemia.
Infection	Break in sterile technique Contaminated catheter moved forward Contaminated IV fluid Prolonged catheter use	See infection control, Pg. 5-18.
Loss of distal perfusion: ↓ or absent pulse, pallor, blanching, cyanosis, mottling, unilateral temp changes, ↑ capillary fill time	Arterial spasm	Usually occurs shortly after insertion and is of short duration. Treatment - inject lidocaine locally and into catheter.
	Thrombosis	Arteriotomy and Fogarty catheterization.

Complication	Cause	Preventive Care / Treatment / Notes
Loss of patency	Positional blockage	Change position of extremity.
	Blood clot on catheter tip	Insure steady flow of heparinized infusate. Always aspirate (I-2 ml) before flushing.
		Note: If aspiration fails to produce a blood return — do not flush. Flushing may cause the clot to dislodge and cause embolization.
Neuromuscular injury	Trauma Irritation	Remove catheter. Assess patient for numbness, pain or tingling. Keep hand (radial) or leg (femoral) in neutral position. Remove catheter if needed.
Fluid overload	Iatrogenic: Excessive fluid administration or stopcock left open	Especially dangerous in CHF or renal failure. Treat with diuretics.
Electric microshock	Improper electric precautions	Observe electrical safety guidelines. Currents < 1 amp may travel via this route.
Pneumothorax	Vessel and pleura puncture during insertion Arterial: Axillary CVP: Subclavian or jugular	Observe closely for distress, perform thoracentesis or insert chest tube as necessary.

Troubleshooting the A-Line

Problem	Possible Causes	Correction/Prevention
Artifact, noise or fling	Catheter whip	Avoid excessive catheter length. Try different tip position.
	Electrical interference	Have Bio-med dept. check.
	Hyperresonance	Dampening device
	Patient movement	Limit patient movement.
Dampened waveform	Air bubbles in system or catheter	Aspirate catheter and/or flush system.
	Blood clot on catheter tip or in system	Aspirate clot with syringe
	Catheter tip against vessel wall	Check for free backflow of blood. Reposition catheter tip if needed.
	Compliant tubing	Use less compliant tubing.
	Improper zero or calibration	Recheck zero and/or calibration.
	Incorrect stopcock position.	Check stopcock position.
	Loose connection	Insure tight connections.
	Loss of counterpressure from bag	Insure proper pressure in pressure bag.
	Loss of IV solution	Replace IV bag.
	Tubing kink	Correct external or internal kinks.
Low reading	Incorrect zero and/or calibration	Recheck zero and/or calibration.
	Loose connection	Check connections.
	Transducer level too high (see Pg. 6-16)	Recheck transducer and patient positions
	Altered tip location	Check position under fluoroscope and/or x-ray and reposition.

Blood Pressure

Problem	Possible Causes	Correction/Prevention
High reading	Fast continous flow	Reduce IV flow
	Incorrect zero and/or calibration	Recheck zero and/or calibration
	Transducer level too low (see Pg. 6-16)	Recheck transducer patient positions
	Altered tip location	Check position under fluoroscope and/or x-ray and reposition.
No waveform	Complete occlusion of catheter	Attempt to aspirate clot If can't, remove catheter.
	Incorrect zero and/or calibration	Recheck zero and/or calibration.
	Incorrect monitor settings	Check monitor settings.
	Incorrect pressure range setting	Check monitor settings.
	Kink in catheter	Reposition
	Loose connection	Check all connections.
	Monitor/amplifier off	Switch power on.
	Stopcock off to patient	Adjust stopcock.
Poor infusion of IV or unable to flush	Blood clot at tip	Aspirate clot
	Kink in tubing	Connect external or internal kinks.
	Pressure bag improperly inflated	Inflate pressure bag.
	Stopcock not open	Open stopcock.
	Catheter tip against wall	Reposition catheter.
Waveform drift	Kink in electrical monitoring cable	Replace cable.
	IV solution temperature change	Allow for temperature equilibration.

Removal of A-Line ①

General —

 Strict aseptic technique is required.

 Know and understand correct procedure.

 Be aware of complications.

 Explain procedure to patient.

Equipment —

 Sterile: gauze sponges, gloves, iodophor ointment, nonallergenic tape, suture removal kit, towels or drapes.

Procedure —

1. Position patient and remove dressing.
2. Remove any sutures.
3. Turn off flush solution.
4. Withdraw catheter rapidly while firmly applying pressure with a sterile pad at insertion site. (It is commonly recommended that a physician remove a femoral line.)
5. Maintain pressure for 5-10 minutes or until bleeding stops. Increase holding time for patients with increased bleeding tendency. For radial site — may elevate arm.
6. Clean site, apply iodophor and a sterile pressure dressing.
7. Remove sterile dressing after 10 minutes and assess site (a sandbag is often placed on a femoral site and left for 2 hours).

> Watch for: bleeding, bruising, motor and sensory use of limb, signs of infection or swelling, distal pulse and limb temperature.

8. If bleeding persists, reapply pressure for another 5-10 minutes. Notify physician if further complications develop.
9. Clean site, apply iodophor ointment and cover with sterile dressing.
10. Recheck site after 1 hour and 4 hours.
11. Document removal and patient assessment.

① General guidelines only. Follow hospital protocol. Removal procedures are basically the same for different sites.

Blood Pressure

6 Central Venous Pressure Monitoring

CENTRAL VENOUS PRESSURE MONITORING

Definition — Monitoring of hemodynamic parameters via a catheter placed in a central venous location (IVC, SVC, RA)

CVP = Central venous pressure
= Pressure in proximal IVC, SVC or RA
≈ RAP (RA filling pressure)
≈ RVEDP (RV filling pressure)

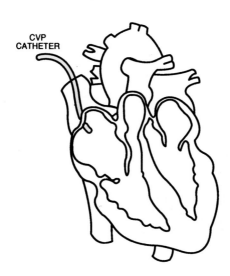

CVP
CATHETER

INDICATIONS FOR CVP MONITORING

Indications	Clinical Notes
Assess cardiac function:	
Right heart	Monitor pressure: CVP ① ≈ $\overline{RAP}$ ≈ RVEDP ② ≈ RH function
	Assess function: RVEDP ≈ RH function
	↑ or ↓ CVP (see Pg. 6-18)
	Note: Normal CVP does *not* rule out circulatory disease or disorder.
Left heart	LH Function: CVP ≈ $\overline{RAP}$ ≈ RVEDP ≈ PAWP ≈ $\overline{LAP}$ ≈ LVEDP ≈ LH function
	CVP ≈ LH function: **only** if no CV disease and not critically ill
	CVP may be normal in presence of LH dysfunction.
	(Pulmonary edema usually becomes well established prior to pressure changes in the RH.)
	① CVP is inaccurate when L-R shunt or restrictive/constrictive cardiomyopathy.
	② CVP ≠ RVEDP when tricuspid insufficiency or stenosis exists.
	In a patient with normal heart and lungs:
	$$RVEDP = \frac{LVEDP - 2 \text{ mmHg}}{2} \text{ or } LVEDP = 2\,RVEDP + 2 \text{ mmHg}$$

Indications	Clinical Notes
Assess intravascular volume status and venous return	CVP ≈ venous return ① ≈ CO ≈ LVEDP ≈ BP (in the absence of CV disease)

Venous return is determined by BP – CVP:

$\downarrow VR = BP - \uparrow CVP$ or $\downarrow BP - CVP$	$\uparrow VR = BP - \downarrow CVP$ or $\uparrow BP - CVP$

| Fluid and drug administration | **Fluids**
 General rule: CVP < 5 cmH$_2$O indicates a need for additional fluid.
 Drugs
 All drugs, except nitroglycerine, can be infused via the CVP line (IV nitroglycerine needs a shorter line due to absorption by the PVC tubing. Be sure all drugs are compatible. The large vein allows for dilution of caustic or hypertonic solutions which would normally cause irritation, local neurosis, pain or phlebitis in smaller veins. |

6-5

Indications	Clinical Notes
Emergency temporary pacemaker route	① CVP ≠ venous return when: 1) PPV with falsely ↑ CVP 2) ↑ venous tone (drugs) **CLINICAL NOTE** Most commonly the CVP is utilized in younger patients with normal heart function. Patients with preexisting CV disease or older patients require more sophisticated monitoring (ie: PA catheter).

CVP Insertion Sites

Note: Site selection is most dependent on inserter's preference and experience, patient's needs and individual considerations.

Site	Advantages	Disadvantages
Neck veins: External jugular	Easily accessible Easily compressed if bleeding Easily observed Fewer complications Large vein	Difficult to secure catheter and dressing Difficult passage into RA. Increased risks for: air embolus, arterial puncture, malposition, pneumothorax, site contamination, thrombosis Low venous flow rates Neck mobility
Internal jugular	Easily accessible Easily compressed if bleeding Easily observable Easy site for correct placement Fewer risks than external jugular High venous flow rates Large vein Short, direct access to RA. Best site for emergency transvenous pacing	Difficult to secure catheter and dressing Neck mobility Risk of air embolus, carotid artery puncture and pneumothorax Trendelenburg position required
Chest vein: Subclavian	Direct route to RA. Easily accessible Easy to secure catheter and dressing Large vein Rapid venous flow rates Remains open during shock Unrestricted patient movement	Difficult to apply pressure during bleed Increased risk of arterial puncture, catheter misplacement, hemo/pneumothorax esp. in patient with COPD or on MV with PEEP

Site	Advantages	Disadvantages

Arm vein:
  Antecubital
  Fossa:
    Cephalic
    Basilic
    Median
    cubital
	Easily accessible.
	Easily compressed if bleeding.
	Easily observable.
	Easy to secure catheter and dressing.
	Low risk of complications.
	Preferred route during CPR.
		Arm immobility.
		Difficult to insert if edematous or hypo-volemic.
		Fluoroscopy often needed for correct placement.
		Guide wire may be needed for cephalic.
		Long catheter required.
		Low venous flow rate
		Small veins (limited reuse)

Leg vein: Femoral	Large and easy to cannulate even during shock.	Decreased patient mobility. Difficult to: apply pressure during bleed, detect bleeding or infiltrate, secure catheter and dressing. Fluoroscopy may be needed for correct placement. Increased risk of arterial puncture, catheter misplacement, infection, pulmonary embolus, thrombosis.

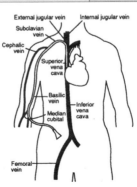

Equipment for Monitoring

Except for a different catheter, the monitoring equipment is the same as for A-lines (see Pg. 5-10).

Equipment Assembly and Calibration

Same as for A-lines (see Pg. 5-12).

CVP Catheter Types

Single lumen

Multi lumen

    Advantages:
        Administer blood or blood products,
           hyperalimentation solutions, incompatible
           drugs simultaneously
        Phlebotomy
        Withdraw venous blood samples

CVP Insertion Techniques

Percutaneous —   Advantages:
                  Less risk of infection
                  More rapid access

Cutdown —   Alternate method for:
                  Collapsed veins (hypovolemia or shock)
                  Children

Percutaneous Insertion Technique

Note: Following procedure is informational only — follow hospital protocol.

Procedure

1. Explain procedure to patient.
2. Prepare monitoring equipment (see Pg. 5-10).
3. Use aseptic technique.
4. Surgically prep and drape insertion site.
   (Cleanse skin with iodine antiseptic or chlorhexidine for one minute and let dry. Then apply 70% alcohol and let dry.)

5. Inserter must wear cap, gown, gloves and mask. Assistants must wear cap and mask.

6. Position patient —
   For jugular or subclavian: patient should be supine or Trendelenburg (maximum upright of 30°). Proper positioning is necessary to prevent occurrence of air embolism.
   Turn head opposite to insertion site with chin upward.
   For subclavian: Place a rolled towel under patient's back, between scapulae.

7. Infiltrate local area with an anesthetic agent (xylocaine 2% or bupivacaine).

8. For subclavian or jugular: Have patient hold breath at end expiration at moment of insertion (and whenever tubing is disconnected from catheter hub). This maneuver increases intrathoracic pressure and helps prevent air entry into bloodstream.

9. Apply constant negative pressure with a syringe as the needle advances.
   Dark blood should appear as needle enters vein.
   Bright red blood indicates arterial puncture — withdraw immediately and hold pressure on site for 5-10 minutes.

10. Attach heparinized flush line and monitor pressure and waveform to determine proper tip positioning.

11. Infuse IV solution (20-30 ml/hr) until x-ray confirmation of position is obtained.
    Do not infuse blood, blood products, lipids, TPN or large volumes until position is confirmed.

12. Confirm position with x-ray, pressure waveform, catheter length, and O_2 sat [high if in left atrium (LA) via F.O.]
    Tip position: is 3-5 cm proximal to caval-atria junction in SVC or distal inominate.

13. Check x-ray for possible pneumothorax (jugular or subclavian insertion).

14. Suture catheter in place and cover with antibiotic/germicidal and sterile gauze dressing.

15. Document procedure and results.

Surgical Cutdown — beyond the scope of this book

Maintenance of CVP line

See Maintenance of A-line, Pg. 5-16.

Drawing a Blood Sample from a CVP Line

Same as A-line (see Pg. 5-19) with following exceptions:

Patient should be flat (or as flat as possible) when withdrawing from the jugular or subclavian vessels.

Blank sample (1st one) should be larger than with A-line (minimum 7 ml) due to longer catheter.

If CVP line is infusing a medication:

Do not interrupt delivery of medication if it is a vasoactive or antiarrhythmic drug.

If OK to interrupt delivery: use a separate solution to flush after sample obtained. Do not flush with the drug solution.

CVP Measurement

Estimation:	by neck veins (Pg. 6-12)
	by hand veins (Pg. 6-14)
Via Catheter:	Water manometer technique (Pg. 6-15)
	Transducer monitoring technique (Pg. 6-16)

Estimation of CVP by Neck Veins

Place patient at 45° angle (semi-Fowlers). (Note angle on chart if different.)

Examine neck for distension and/or pulsation of internal or external jugular veins.① (next page)

no distension/pulsation	completely distended/ no pulsations
lower patient's head until see crest of vein distension or pulsation	raise patient's head until see crest of vein distension or pulsation

Measure in centimeters the vertical distance between top (crest) of vein distension/pulsation and estimated level of middle of RA (phlebostatic axis) ② (next page)

centimeter distance = CVP in cmH₂0

10 cm

5 cm

0 cm   Sternum angle

5 cm

Mid-right atrium

Estimation of central venous pressure using the vertical distance from the sternal angle to the pulsating crest of the internal jugular vein.

① **External Jugular Vein**

Normal distension:

45° angle — crest of vein column is just superior to mid-clavicle.

> **Note:** Gentle compression of superior border of mid-clavicle allows filling of vein for easy identification of the vein.

Supine — full length of vein is distended.

> **Note:** Collapse in the supine position suggests hypovolemia.

Internal Jugular Vein

The vein column is deep in the neck and distension cannot be seen visually, but the skin pulsation may be seen at the level of the column crest.

> **Note:** The right internal jugular vein gives the most accurate estimate of CVP.

Distinguishing a Jugular Pulse from a Carotid Pulse	
Jugular Pulse	**Carotid Pulse**
Often visible	Not clearly visible
Disappears on palpation	Palpable
Disappears when upright	Does not change with position
Disappears with pressure above clavicle	No change with pressure above clavicle
Crest level drops with deep inspiration	Crest level unchanged with deep inspiration

② Estimation of phlebostatic axis: Measure vertical distance (in cm) between crest of distension/pulsation and sternal angle (angle of Louis), then add 5 cm. Total cm = CVP in cm H_2O. (See also Pg. 6-16)

Clinical Situations Affecting Neck Vein Assessment
Decreased perfusion states
Inability to raise patient's head
Increased intrathoracic pressure:
COPD with expiratory obstruction
PPV and/or PEEP/CPAP
Marked distension from very high venous pressures
Obstructed SVC (intrathoracic tumor)
Short thick necks
Trauma, surgery, dressings in neck area

Estimation of CVP by Hand Veins

Position patient at 30°.
Position arm dependently so that dorsal hand veins distend.
Raise arm slowly.
If veins collapse:
    Before level of sternal angle =   low venous pressure
    At level of sternal angle =   normal venous pressure
    Above level of sternal angle =   high venous pressure

CLINICAL NOTE
Estimation of CVP can be used to check the accuracy of a high reading from an indwelling catheter.

Measurement of CVP via Catheter

Water Manometer Technique: (Rarely used today).

Position patient supine without pillow if possible. (If supine is contra-indicated or intolerable, lower as much as possible, preferably under 30°). ①

Calibrate manometer stand to zero: Place zero point on manometer level with the phlebostatic axis. ② (May use a carpenter's level. Mark patient's chest for future reference.)

Check IV line to insure free flow. Ⓐ

Turn stopcock off to patient and open to manometer. Ⓑ

Fill manometer to 10cmH$_2$O greater than suspected CVP.

Turn stopcock off to IV flow (open between patient and manometer). Ⓒ

Observe drop in fluid level. CVP pressure equals the stabilized level at end-expiration. (Read bottom of meniscus or ball midline.)

> [Fluctuation is normal during spontaneous inspiration ($\downarrow$ I, $\uparrow$ E).
> PPV may $\rightarrow$ $\uparrow$ CVP during I and $\downarrow$ CVP during E.
> Removal from PPV and/or PEEP is usually not advised.
>   See Pg. 7-38]

Turn stopcock off to manometer. Resume IV flow to patient. Ⓓ

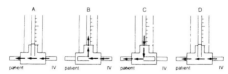

Convert observed cmH$_2$O level to mmHg and record. (See Pg. 6-17 or 1 cmH$_2$O = 0.74 mmHg or divide cmH$_2$O by 1.36).

Establish a base reading by measuring q15 minutes × 4 measurements. (Remember, serial trends are more clinically significant than one isolated reading.)

---

① Each and every reading should be taken with the patient in the same position.

② Phlebostatic axis = approximate level of right atrium = midaxillary point on lateral chest, nipple line in 4th intercostal space.

Transducer Monitoring Technique

Insure transducer is zeroed and calibrated (see Pg. 5-12).

Position patient supine without pillow. (If supine is contraindicated or intolerable, lower as much as possible, preferably under 30°). Each and every reading should be taken with the patient in the same position.

Insure transducer is level with phlebostatic axis.① (May use a carpenter's level for pole transducers. Newer transducers may be attached to the patient's upper arm at level of RA. Mark patient's chest for future reference.)

---

① Phlebostatic axis = approximate level of right atrium
= midaxillary point on lateral chest, nipple line, in 4th intercostal space.

Note:

Transducer level		*Reading*
Each cm above phlebostatic point	→	↓ 1.86 mmHg < true (false low)
Each cm below phlebostatic point	→	↑ 1.86 mmHg > true (false high)

CVP Interpretation

Pressures:

CVP = 0-6 mmHg (normal value)
      (0-8 cmH$_2$O) ① See table below.

CVP = mean RAP ② (RA filling pressure)

CVP ≈ RVEDP ③ (RV filling pressure) ≈ RH function ④

CLINICAL NOTE

Trends are more clinically important than absolute values.
Never interpret CVP alone without assessing clinical
parameters also. Subsequent reading should not differ more
than 2 cmH$_2$O.

Pressure is the same in children.

① Most measurements today are expressed in mmHg.
② No systolic or diastolic pressures are recorded.
   All measurements are made at end expiration.
③ Assuming no functional obstruction between the RA and RV.
④ CVP is not a reliable indicator of LV function.

CONVERSION OF:

cmH$_2$O → mmHg	mmHg → cmH$_2$O
$\dfrac{cmH_2O}{1.36} = mmHg$	$mmHg \times 1.36 = cmH_2O$

mm Hg		cm H$_2$O
0	=	0*
1	=	1
2	=	3
3	=	4
4	=	5
5	=	7
6	=	8
7	=	10
8	=	11
9	=	12
10	=	14
11	=	15
12	=	16
13	=	18
14	=	19
15	=	20

*cm H$_2$O
reported in
nearest whole
number.

PRESSURE VARIATIONS

Pressure Change	Potential Causes		
↑ CVP	**↑ Preload:** Fluid overload L → R shunt (VSD) Valular insufficiency: tricuspid **↓ Contractility:** Cardiac tamponade Cardiomyopathy Constrictive pericarditis LVF → ↑ RVEDP Myocardial infarct (esp. RH) Myocarditis RVF	**↑ Afterload:** Chronic LVF Cor pulmonale Pulmonary — ↑ PVR: pulmonary embolism, pulmonary hypertension, pulmonic stenosis, COPD, ARDS, hypoxemia. ↑ PIT: PPV esp. with Peep **Other:** Tricuspid stenosis Tip migrated into RV Positional change in patient or transducer Clot in line	**Normal:** During spontaneous expiration During positive pressure inspiration
↓ CVP	**Hypovolemia** Absolute - blood loss/H₂O loss Relative - excessive vaso or venodilation shock	**Other:** Positional change in patient or transducer	**Normal:** During spontaneous inspiration During positive pressure expiration

6-18

CVP Waveform ① & ②

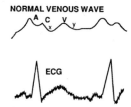

Waveform part	Description	EKG correlate
a wave	RA contraction (atrial systole or kick, ventricular diastole)	immediately following P wave
c wave	Closure of tricuspid valve (begin ventricular systole)	RS-T junction
v wave	Filling of RA and bulging of tricuspid valve into RA (ventricular systole) (often not seen)	T-P interval
x descent	Downward slope of a wave (RA relaxation)	
y descent	Downward slope of v wave (RV relaxation and RA emptying)	

① CVP waveform is identical to RA waveform. (See Pg. 2-10.) Waveform is similar for LA and PAWP waveform, Pg. 2-11.

CVP:	a wave > v wave
PAWP:	a wave < v wave

② *Waveform is the same in children.*

CVP Waveform Variations

Variation	Physiologic event	Pathological causes
Prominent a wave (exaggerated)	↑ RA contraction	Pulmonary hypertension Tricuspid stenosis
	↑ Resistance to RV filling	Above two plus: Pulmonary valve stenosis RVF
15— 0—	RA contraction against a closed tricuspid valve (canon wave)	a-v dissociation 3rd° heart block
Absent a wave 10—	↓ or absent atrial contraction	Atrial fibrillation Junctional arrhythmias Ventricular pacing
Prominent v wave (exaggerated)	↑ Blood volume (pressure) in RA during RV contraction	Tricuspid regurgitation
25—	↑ Blood volume (pressure) in RV during RV contraction	RVF ↓ RV compliance
Prominent a and v wave 15— (Xy) or (xY)	↑ EDP in all heart chambers	Cardiac tamponade (Xy)① Constrictive pericarditis xY② Acute RV infarct } or xy Hypervolemia

① Xy = predominant X descent with a short or absent y descent.
    xY = predominant y descent.
    xy = x and y descents are equal.

② Kussmaul sign = ↑ venous pressure during inspiration rather than expiration. (Not seen in cardiac tamponade.)

CVP COMPLICATIONS TO WATCH FOR

Same as A-line (see Pg. 5-28) plus:

Complication	Cause	Preventive Care / Treatment / Notes
Arrhythmias	Spontaneous migration of catheter into RV	Often occurs suddenly when turning the patient.
		Reposition patient to former position.
		Most common arrhythmias are PVCs and V-tach.
		Obtain X-ray, when position is in doubt.
Perforation of cardiac chamber	Catheter migration or advancement	Stop IV infusion immediately, and remove catheter.
		Treat for cardiac tamponade:
		Signs and symptoms, see Pg. 10-9.
		Treatment, see Pg. 10-10.

Troubleshooting the CVP Line

Same as A-line (see Pg. 5-31).
Plus:

Problem	Possible Causes	Correction
Fluctuations	Respirations	Normal
	Heart beat	Abnormal — tip has migrated into the RV.
	Positive pressure ventilation	Insure readings are taken in a consistent manner (ie., end expiration).

Removal of CVP Catheter

Same as A-line (see Pg. 5-33), with following difference:

Place patient supine if CVP is in the jugular or subclavian veins.

PAP

continued next page

Chapter Contents

Overview of Ventilatory Effects on Hemodynamic Pressures

Definition

Monitoring① of hemodynamic parameters via a catheter② placed in a pulmonary artery.

PA	=	pulmonary artery
PAP	=	pulmonary artery pressures
PADP	=	pulmonary artery diastolic pressure (same as PAEDP)
PAMP	=	mean pulmonary artery pressure
PASP	=	pulmonary artery systolic pressure
PAWP (PCWP, PAOP)	=	pulmonary artery wedge pressure

PAP

① Provides rapid, beat-to-beat information of hemodynamic status.
② Swan-Ganz® or flow-directed.

Indications for PAP Monitoring ①	
Indications	**Clinical Notes**
Assess cardiac function:	
Right Heart	<u>Monitor Pressures:</u> CVP② ≈ $\overline{RAP}$ ≈ RVEDP③ ≈ RH function (See also Pg. 6-17). RVSP ≈ PASP (see Pg. 7-18) <u>Assess RH function:</u> RVEDP ≈ RH function Pulmonary and tricuspid valve function
Left Heart	<u>Monitor Pressures:</u> CVP ≈ $\overline{RAP}$ ≈ RVEDP ≈ PADP ≈ PAWP ≈ $\overline{LAP}$ ≈ LVEDP ≈ LV function (See Pg. 7-18). <u>Assess LH function:</u> LAP ≈ LVEDP ≈ LV function (see Pg. 7-18) Aortic and tricuspid valve function <u>Measure</u> Cardiac Output and SVR
Assess pulmonary function	<u>Monitor Pressures:</u> PASP, PADP, PAMP, PAWP <u>Monitor Flow</u> PVR Shunts <u>Measure</u> $P\overline{v}O_2$ $S\overline{v}O_2$

① There are no absolute contraindications, but the benefit must be weighed against potential complications. PA catheters may be used with extreme caution in patients with: anticoagulant therapy, bleeding tendencies, hypercoaguable states, immunosuppression, recurrent sepsis.

② CVP is inaccurate when L-R shunt or restrictive/constrictive cardiomyopathy.

③ CVP ≠ RVEDP when tricuspid insufficiency or stenosis exists.

Indications	Clinical Notes
Diagnosis, management and treatment of:	
Heart disorders	Cardiac surgery, Constrictive pericarditis, Cardiac tamponade, Cardiogenic shock, Cor pulmonale, Congenital heart disease, MI, CHF, Shock, Shunts (intracardiac), Valve dysfunction
Lung disorders	ARDS COPD (acute exacerbation) Pulmonary edema Pulmonary emboli Shunts (Intrapulmonary)
Other	Drug intoxication Hemorrhagic pancreatitis High risk obstetric patient Major cardiac or vascular surgery Patients on circulatory assist device Patients on PPV with PEEP < 10 cmH$_2$O Sepsis
Assess blood volume status	<u>Monitor fluid requirements:</u> Burns, Sepsis Hypovolemia, Trauma Renal failure <u>Monitor fluid replacement therapy</u>
Monitor therapeutic interventions	Oxygen, fluid and drug administration

CLINICAL NOTE

Secondary uses of the PA catheter, once it is in place, include:

Cardiac pacing
Central blood temperature monitoring
Injection of dye for pulmonary angiograms

PA Catheter Insertion Sites

Same as CVP insertion sites (see Pg. 6-7).

Equiment for Monitoring

Except for a different catheter, the monitoring equipment is the same as for A-lines (see Pg. 5-10).

Equipment Assembly and Calibration

Same as A-line (see Pg. 5-12).

PA Catheter Types

There are numerous types available, but the most common is the quadruple lumen, thermodilution catheter:

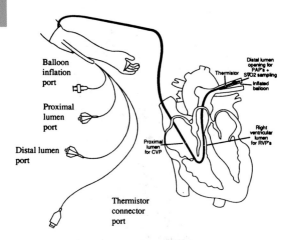

Balloon inflation port

Proximal lumen port

Distal lumen port

Thermistor connector port

Distal lumen opening for PAP's + STO2 sampling

Thermistor

Inflated balloon

Right ventricular lumen for RVP's

Proximal lumen for CVP

CLINICAL NOTE

Do not administer drugs and/or caustic or hyperosmotic solutions through the distal (PA) port.

Do not infuse vasoactive drugs in proximal (RA) port if CO studies are to be done.

General Protocol:

Insure patient and family consent, teaching and preparation.

Know and understand the manufacturer's directions.

Insertion should be performed or supervised by an experienced physician.

Insertion personnel should be dressed in full surgical scrub.

Assisting personnel should wear caps and masks.

Patient should wear mask, if appropriate.

Clinical assessment of patient is essential prior to and during insertion.

Monitor vital signs and EKG, closely.

Insure CPR equipment, including a defibrillator, is immediately available.

Insertion Preparation *(General guidelines only; follow hospital protocol.)*

1. **Testing of PA catheter balloon.**
   1. *Inflate balloon.*
      Inflate with air to manufacturer's recommended volume (indicated on shaft).
      Never use fluids to inflate balloon.
   2. *Inspect* balloon for shape and symmetry.
      Balloon should protrude over, but not cover, the tip.
   3. *Check* for leaks.
      Submerge in sterile H_2O or saline, and look for small air bubbles.
   4. *Deflate* balloon.
      Allow balloon to passively deflate by simply removing syringe from port.
      Do *not* use negative pressure with a syringe.
      Insure fully deflated before insertion. This insures against overinflation.

2. **If thermodilution PA catheter:**
   Check thermistor wires by connecting CO cable to catheter connection. CO computer will flash "faulty" if wires are damaged. Replace catheter if damaged.

3. **If SvO₂ PA catheter:**
   Calibrate fiberoptics (see manufacturer's directions).

4. **Prepare catheter:**
   Connect stopcocks, flush, and fill proximal and distal lumens with heparinized solution and close stopcocks.

PAP

Lubricate the outside of the catheter with sterile water or saline.

Attach distal port stopcock to flush solution.

Connect to transducer and monitor.

5. **Establish vascular access.**

    Percutaneous technique — most common for internal jugular or subclavian veins. Usually less risk of infection.

    Cutdown technique — most common for basilic or cephalic veins. (Not covered in this text. See hospital protocol.)

Percutaneous Insertion Technique

(General guidelines only; follow hospital protocol.)

1. Explain procedure to patient.
2. Prepare monitoring equipment (see Pg. 5-12).
3. Use aseptic technique.
4. Surgically prep and drape insertion site. (Cleanse skin with iodine antiseptic or chlorhexidine for one minute and let dry. Then apply 70% alcohol and let dry.)
5. Inserter must wear cap, gown, gloves and mask. Assistants must wear cap and mask.
6. Position patient —

    For jugular or subclavian: patient should be supine or Trende-lenburg (maximum upright of 30°). Proper positioning is necessary to prevent occurrence of air embolism. Turn head opposite to insertion site with chin upward.

    For subclavian: Place a rolled towel under patient's back, between scapulae.
7. Infiltrate local area with an anesthetic agent (xylocaine 2% or bupivacaine).
8. For subclavian or jugular: Have patient hold breath at end expiration at moment of insertion (and whenever tubing is disconnected from catheter hub). This manueuver increases intrathoracic pressure and helps prevent air entry into bloodstream.
9. Apply constant negative pressure with a syringe as the needle advances.
10. Introduce catheter with balloon deflated.

     Watch entire catheter length during insertion to insure against contamination.
11. Gently aspirate distal (PA) lumen to insure free flow of blood, then flush.

12. Turn stopcock to open distal (PA) lumen for pressure and waveform monitoring during the insertion procedure.
13. Monitor closely for arrhythmias.

Average Distance

to RA	From
10 cm	Subclavian
10-15 cm	ⓡ Internal jugular
30-40 cm	ⓡ Antecubital fossa
40-50 cm	ⓛ Antecubital fossa
35-45 cm	Femoral

15. Inflate balloon:

Balloon should be inflated to manufacturer's recommended volume (use supplied, restricted volume or a tuberculin syringe for accurate volumes). Do **not** float catheter with less than recommended volume unless justified by tricuspid or pulmonic stenosis.

Some clinicians inflate balloon, before RA, when entering a central or thoracic vein (ie: balloon is inflated immediately after entering internal jugular, subclavian, or femoral).

Respiratory fluctuations or marked deflections during a cough indicate the tip has entered a thoracic vein.

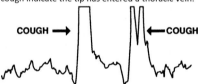

COUGH ➡   ⬅ COUGH

Use CO_2 when R-L shunts are suspected. (Note: CO_2 diffuses out of balloon at a rate of 0.5 ml/min.)

16. Advance (float) catheter through heart and into pulmonary vessels:

Fluoroscopy may be required.

Monitor pressures and waveforms as each region is traversed (see table on Pg. 7-11).

(Remember, patients requiring PA catheters may have cardiopulmonary dysfunction and hence abnormal values.)

Watch for cardiac arrhythmias, tachypnea, dyspnea, hemoptysis, or any change in vital signs.

17. Once balloon reaches PA occlusion position (note resistance to advancement and PAWP waveform), the balloon should not remain inflated more than 15 seconds, or 5 breaths.

    (In addition to the risk of ischemia to the lung, prolonged wedging may result in false high pressure from tip occlusion by the balloon or vessel wall.)
18. Deflate balloon:

> **Note:** Do not aspirate air out of balloon. Open valve and allow passive deflation. Keep port level lower than heart level. Keep open only for a few seconds.

    Upon deflation, the PA waveform should reappear immediately. (If wedge waveform continues, the catheter should be carefully pulled back.)
19. Suture catheter in place. Dress site with iodophor ointment and cover with a sterile dressing.
20. Verify absence of pneumothorax and correct position of tip with X-ray. (Tip of catheter should not extend beyond silhouette of mediastinal structures.)

> **Note:** If tip is too distal into peripheral circulation:
> 1. Catheter may spontaneously wedge.
> 2. Catheter tip may damage pulmonary vasculature.
> 3. CO measurements may be in error.
> 4. Mixed venous samples may contain some arterialized blood.

21. Document procedure, patient assessment, pressures and waveforms in patient's chart, type catheter used, complications, and balloon volume used.

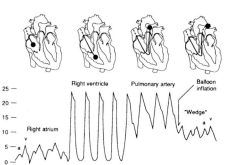

Normal Pressure and Waveform Characteristics as PA Catheter is Advanced		
Location	**Pressure**	**Waveform Characteristics** *(see Fig.above).*
RA	$\overline{RAP}$ = 0-6 mmHg	Low amplitude, continuous baseline oscillation. a wave = RVEDP v wave = RA filling
RV	RVSP = 15-25 mmHg RVEDP = 0-6 mmHg	Steep upstroke to peak RVSP Sharp downstroke to RVEDP No dicrotic notch
PA	PASP = 15-25 mmHg = RVSP	Steep upstroke to peak PASP Sharp downstroke to PADP Dicrotic notch is Present
	PADP = 8-15 mmHg > RVEDP	
	PAMP = 10-15 mmHg = $\dfrac{PASP + 2PADP}{3}$	
	PAWP = 4-12 mmHg ≈ PADP - (0-6 mmHg) = $\overline{PVP}$ ≈ LAP/LVEDP	Low amplitude, oscillation (LA waveform) a wave = LVEDP v wave = LA filling

Wedging Protocol

Slowly inflate balloon while observing PA waveform.
Stop inflation when PA waveform changes to PAWP waveform.

Note: Inflate with the restricted volume syring provided or a tuberculin syringe for accurate volumes and never add more than recommended (usually < 1.5 cc). Inflation beyond this point may lead to PA damage or overinflated balloon. A wedge obtained with *less than recommended* volume suggests peripheral migration of the catheter.

Record mean PAWP at end expiration (see Pg. 7-26).
Deflate balloon within 15 seconds or maximum of 5 breaths.
PA waveform should reappear immediately.

Note: Allow passive deflation of balloon by opening valve.
Do not aspirate the air.

Verifying a True Wedge Position

1. Upon balloon inflation — PA waveform flattens to an LA waveform. (See Pg. 7-11)
    Upon balloon deflation — PA waveform reappears.
2. PAWP is always < PADP or PAMP.
    (If PAWP > PADP = artifact)
3. Blood sample:
    Blood withdrawn from the distal port of a wedged catheter is always highly saturated with O_2.

Note: This procedure is only done when catheter position is in doubt.

Procedure:

1. Inflate balloon.
2. Draw first sample — 2 ml (all from distal lumen). Discard.
3. Draw second sample — 2 ml. Label PAWP for analysis.
4. Deflate balloon.
5. Draw third sample — 2 ml (very slowly: 1 ml/20 sec). Discard.
6. Draw fourth sample — 2 ml (very slowly: 1 ml/ 20 sec). Label PA for analysis.
7. Analyze samples 2 and 4.

> PAWP blood (2nd sample) should be 100% sat.
> PA blood (4th sample) should be ≈ 75% sat.

Expected alterations in O_2 sat:

$\downarrow$ PAWP O_2 SAT = significant shunting (atelectasis or consolidation) or PEEP

$\uparrow$ PA O_2 SAT = rapid aspiration.

Guidelines to Prevent Balloon Rupture

Inflate slowly.
>Do not inflate with fluid.
>Never use greater than recommended volume.
>Stop inflation when wedge tracing is obtained.

Do not advance catheter with balloon deflated.

Minimize wedge time (< 15 sec.).

Minimize number of wedges.
>Use PADP, if possible, to assess PAWP, LAP and LVEDP (see Pg. 7-18).

Do not irrigate forcefully.

Do not deflate balloon with negative pressure (syringe).
Always allow passive deflation.

Checking for Balloon Rupture

Inflate balloon using a glass syringe. Barrel will spring back when released if balloon is intact.
If rupture has occurred, see Complications, Pg. 7-40.

Maintenance of PA Line

General guidelines. See A-line (Pg. 5-14).

Specific Guidelines

A chest X-ray should be obtained daily (to check placement and zone) or stat if catheter seems displaced.

IV solutions, meds and blood products should only be infused via the proximal port.
(Distal port may be used for emergency IV, if no other central line available or to infuse pulmonary vasodilators.)

Always verify proper tip placement by <u>continuous</u> monitoring of the distal lumen waveform.

Insure all measurements and tracings are done consistently: Same position, same reference point, same part of respiratory cycle (see Pg. 7-26).

Check PAWP and waveform q 2-4 hours.

Insure balloon fully deflated following wedging.

Patients with PA catheters should be kept on bed rest.

(See S$\bar{v}O_2$ Monitoring, Pg. 3-8.)

1. Insure PA catheter tip is properly positioned with balloon deflated.

2. Use aseptic technique.

3. Prepare blood gas syringe:
   Heparinize syringe (see A-line, Pg. 5-19)

4. Remove sterile cap from the distal port of the PA catheter (place in sterile gauze) and attache a 10 ml syringe.

5. Turn stopcock off to flush solution and on to patient.

6. Gently (< 3 ml/min) withdraw 5 ml of blood or until clear line of flush solution.

7. Turn stopcock off to all three ports, remove syringe and discard.

8. Attach the blood gas syringe (3-5cc heparinized).

9. Turn stopcock on to patient, slowly and gently withdraw desired amount of blood (2-3cc). Rapid aspiration will contaminate the sample with capillary blood, resulting in a false increase in S$\bar{v}O_2$.

10. Close stopcock and remove syringe and prepare for ABG analysis (see A-line, Pg. 5-19).

> **NOTE:** S$\bar{v}O_2$ should be measured directly by a CO-oximeter rather than being calculated from P$\bar{v}O_2$. The latter is often unreliable due to wide changes in the P50.

11. Attach a new sterile syringe to stopcock. Open to flush solution and irrigate line until stopcock is clear.

12. Turn stopcock off, remove and discard syringe.

13. Replace sterile cap.

14. Turn stopcock on to patient and flush line for 1-3 seconds.

15. Resume flow of flush solution.

16. Check for the presence of proper PA waveform.

PAP

(See S$\bar{v}$O$_2$ monitoring, Pg. 3-8.)

Operation & Troubleshooting the S$\bar{v}$O$_2$ Monitor
  (see manufacturer's manual)

Common Errors to Watch For

Technical	Abnormal light intensity signals
	Catheter tip position ($\uparrow$ S$\bar{v}$O$_2$ may indicate tip against wall)
	Erroneous blood sample for calibration
	Fibrin deposition on optic tip
	Improper calibration
	Perform Co-oximetry on a sample if accuracy is in question.
Interpretation	S$\bar{v}$O$_2$ does not correlate well with CO
	A normal S$\bar{v}$O$_2$ does not indicate a normal SvO$_2$ from any individual vascular bed.
	Caution when interpreting high values (> 80%) Severe Mitral regurgitation may cause a falsely elevated S$\bar{v}$O$_2$.

PAP

Procedure:

Insure correct patient position (see Pg. 6-16).

Insure correct transducer position (see Pg. 6-16).

Insure correct catheter tip placement (see Pg. 7-30).

Insure monitor system properly zeroed and calibrated (see Pg. 5-12)

PAP

> **Note:** Inaccurate information may lead to improper management. Always use other clinical assessments in conjunction with hemodynamic parameters.

Single quartz transducer for continuous PA pressure monitoring and intermittent RA pressure monitoring.

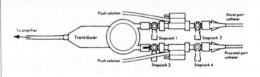

Continuous PAP monitoring: Stopcocks 1, 2 and 4 are open.
Stopcock 3 is closed.

Intermittent $\overline{\text{RAP}}$ monitoring: Stopcock 1 is closed.
Stopcocks 2, 3 and 4 are open.

Measured (Implied)	Derived
CO	CI
CVP	CvO_2
HR	$C\bar{v}O_2$
PADP	LV
PASP	function curve
PAWP (LAP, LVEDP)	LVSW
pHv	LVSWI
pH$\bar{v}$	PAMP
$PvCO_2$	PVR
$P\bar{v}CO_2$	PVRI
PvO_2	RVSW
$P\bar{v}O_2$	RVSWI
RAP (RVEDP)	SV
SvO_2	SVI
$S\bar{v}O_2$	SW
	SWI

PAP

NOTE: All invasive parameters may be obtained with the combination of an A-line and a PA line (thermodil):

A-line parameters
+
PA line parameters

$\rightarrow$

	Derived	
a-vDO$_2$		$M\dot{v}O_2$
a-$\bar{v}$DO$_2$		$M\dot{D}O_2$
Ca-vO$_2$		O_2ER
Ca-$\bar{v}O_2$		$\dot{Q}S/\dot{Q}T$
CPP		SVR
$\dot{D}O_2$		SVRI
		$\dot{V}O_2$

[1] Thermodilution type

PA Line Interpretations

Pressures: ①

Pressure	Normal Value	Clinical Notes
CVP	0-6 mmHg	See Pg. 6-3
RVSP/ RVEDP	15-25 mmHg 0-6 mmHg	Newer catheters may have an RV port used to monitor for proper catheter tip positioning.
PASP	15-25 mmHg	Systolic pressure in pulmonary vasculature PASP ≈ RVSP PASP ≠ RVSP when have pulmonary stenosis or other RV outflow obstruction (RVSP will be > PASP).
PADP	8-15 mmHg	Diastolic pressure in pulmonary vasculature PADP ≈ PAWP ≈ LAP ≈ LVEDP ≈ LV function Continuous PADP monitoring may be used to monitor LH function, if have normal PVR, normal mitral valve and HR < 125. PADP ≠ PAWP ≠ LAP or LVEDP or LV function when have ↑ PVR (ARDS, COPD, embolus), abnormal mitral valve or HR > 125. (See Pg. 7-20) This monitoring will minimize the # of balloon inflations, hence reducing the risks of PA damage.
PAMP	10-15 mmHg	Mean pressure in pulmonary vasculature $PAMP = \dfrac{PASP + 2PADP}{3}$
PAWP	4-12 mmHg ②	Mean pressure in pulmonary capillaries PAWP ≈ LAP ≈ LVEDP ≈ LV function (See Pg. 7-19,20)
PADP-PAWP gradient	0-6 mmHg	PADP – PAWP gradient ≈ PVR (See Pg. 7-21)

① All pressures should be measured at end-expiration.

② Normally the mean PAWP is recorded (average of a and v waves). Both a and v pressures may be recorded if there is a significant difference.

CAUSES OF ↑ OR ↓ PAP (PASP, PADP, PAMP)

↓ PAP (overall)	↑ PAP (overall)
Hypovolemia	↑ Pulmonary blood volume
Relative (vasodilator	Hypervolemia
therapy, etc.)	L-R shunt (ASD, VSD)
	↑ PVR (pulmonary hypertension, embolism, vasopressors, hypoxemia, acidosis)
Absolute	↑ Pulmonary venous pressure
(dehydration)	LVF
	Mitral stenosis / insufficiency
	Cardiac tamponade

CAUSES OF ↑ OR ↓ PAWP

↓ PAWP (< 4)	↑ PAWP (> 12)
Hypovolemia	Cardiac tamponade
(Note: PAWP may	Constrictive pericarditis
be ↑ if heart is	Hypervolemia
compromised)	LVF
	Mitral regurgitation or stenosis
	↑ Pleural pressure —
	pneumothorax
	PPV

Note: PAWP > 18 → mild pulmonary congestion.
PAWP > 30 → acute pulmonary edema.

Caution: Causes of erroneous pressures:

Rewedging in different part of lung (see Pg. 7-30)
Pseudowedge: PA waveform disappears and
is replaced by a damped tracing resembling a
PAWP waveform.
Overinflation of balloon.
Tip against vessel wall.

Note: *Clinical appearance is not usually relative to PAWP in children. Children are more likely to develop increased pulmonary-capillary permeability and pulmonary edema during respiratory dysfunction. Hence PAWP is often normal despite evidence of pulmonary edema.*

CAUSES FOR PAWP ≠ LAP OR LVEDP OR LV FUNCTION:

PAWP < LVEDP	PAWP > LVEDP
↓ LV compliance or contractility:	HR > 125
Acute MI	Hypovolemia (relative)
Aortic insufficiency	Hypoxemia
Cardiac tamponade	Obstruction between PA and LV:
Constructive pericarditis	Catheter tip in zone 1 or 2
LVF	(see Pg. 7-30)
Mitral regurgitation	LA myxoma
Hypervolemia?	Mitral stenosis
	↑ PA from PPV or CPAP
	Pulmonary disease:
Note: When LVEDP > 25, the pressure is not adequately reflected back.	ARDS
	COPD
	Embolism
	Pulmonary venous obstruction

VERIFYING PAWP ≈ LVEDP

1. Correct patient position (HOB 0-45°)?
   Correct transducer position (phlebostatic axis)?
   Catheter tip in Zone 3 (see Pg. 7-30)?
   Monitor system zeroed and calibrated (see Pg. 5-12).
   No line obstructions (square wave flush, see Pg. 5-17)?
   Correct balloon inflation volume?
   Waveform appropriate?
   Measurement at end-expiration (avg. of three)?

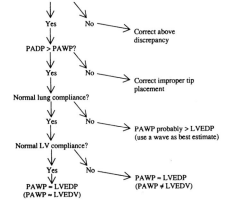

CAUSES OF ↑ OR ↓ PADP - PAWP GRADIENT

↑ Gradient (↑ PVR)	↓ Gradient (↓ PVR)
Pulmonary embolism	Pulmonary vasodilation
Pulmonary hypertension	(usually iatrogenic —
Pulmonary	induced)
vasoconstriction:	
Pulmonary disease —	
ARDS	
COPD	
Acidosis	
Hypoxia	**Note:** PADP < PAWP = negative
Hypercarbia	gradient with backward flow
HR > 125 (false elevation	of blood! More than likely this
of PADP)	represents an overwedged
	catheter tip!

Examples of PADP – PAWP gradient variations

Pressures	Indicative of	Example
↑ PADP – norm PAWP (↑ gradient)	Pulmonary problem ↑ PVR: COPD ARDS Embolus Hypoxia	↑ PADP 30 PAWP 10 ↑ Gradient = 20 (COPD)
↑ PADP – ↑ PAWP (normal gradient)	Heart problem or fluid overload	↑ PADP 26 ↑ PAWP 21 Gradient = 5 (acute MI)
↑ PADP – ↑ PAWP (↑ gradient)	Mixed pulmonary and heart problem	↑ PADP 40 ↑ PAWP 20 ↑ Gradient = 20 (Pulmonary embolism and LVF)

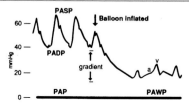

7-21

PA Line Interpretation:

Waveforms: ① Significance — Reflects function and pressure changes in RH, LH and PVR

Waveform	Description
PAP waveform PULMONARY ARTERY: SYSTOLIC 15-25 mmHg DIASTOLIC 8-15 mmHg MEAN 10-15 mmHg	Similar to arterial pressure waveform except 1/6 in size (see also Pg. 2-22 and 5-23) Systole = anacrotic limb plus first part of dicrotic limb down to dicrotic notch Diastole = dicrotic notch to next anacrotic limb Dicrotic notch = closure of pulmonic valve

PAWP waveform

PULMONARY WEDGE
MEAN 4-12 mmHg

PAWP waveform = LAP waveform (similar contour and same pressures)

PAWP waveform ≈ RAP waveform (same contour but PAWP > RAP)

PAWP Waveform

Part	Description	EKG Correlate
a wave	LA contraction (atrial systole or kick, ventricular diastole	Immediately following P wave
c wave	Closure of mitral valve (begin ventricular systole) (often not seen)	RST
v wave	Filling of LA and bulging of mitral valve in LA (ventricular systole)	T-P interval
X descent	Downward slope of a wave (LA relaxation)	
Y descent	Downward slope of v wave (LV relaxation) and LA emptying	

continued

RV waveform

R. VENTRICLE
SYSTOLIC 15-25 mmHg
DIASTOLIC 0-6 mmHg

DIASTOLE **SYSTOLE** DIASTOLE

ECG

Available from a catheter with an RV port. Use to monitor for proper catheter tip position

Catheter tip migration may show a PA waveform from the RV port

① This section deals with waveforms obtained via the distal lumen. See Pg. 6-19 for CVP waveforms via the proximal lumen.

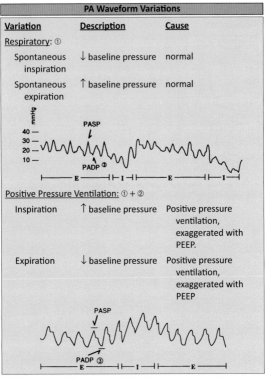

PA Waveform Variations

Variation	Description	Cause
Respiratory: ①		
Spontaneous inspiration	↓ baseline pressure	normal
Spontaneous expiration	↑ baseline pressure	normal

Positive Pressure Ventilation: ① + ②

Variation	Description	Cause
Inspiration	↑ baseline pressure	Positive pressure ventilation, exaggerated with PEEP.
Expiration	↓ baseline pressure	Positive pressure ventilation, exaggerated with PEEP

① The extent of fluctuations is directly proportional to the extent of airway pressure changes. Often up to 10-20 mmHg.

② Pressure fluctuations are dependent on the mode of ventilation (ie: whether the ventilator or patient does most of the work.) Negative spontaneous effort will counteract the positive machine breaths. Hence, each respiratory cycle may be different depending on whether the patient is breathing on their own (simv), assisted (assist control, simv), supported (pressure support), controlled, etc.

③ Point of end-expiration, lowest proximal airway pressure and point of end expiratory flow. (See Pg. 7-26)

Variation	Description	Cause
RV waveform 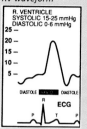	Rectangular shape No dicrotic notch Steep decline in pressure Pressure: $\underline{15\text{-}25}$ mmHg $0\text{-}6$	Catheter tip slipped back into RV

NaN**Note:** PA waveform is:

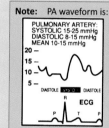

Triangular in shape
Dicrotic notch
Gradual decline in pressure
Pressures: $\underline{15\text{-}25}$ mmHg
$8\text{-}15$

Variation	Description	Cause
Mixed RV and PA waveform	RV waveform appears during diastole	Catheter tip is near pulmonic valve
	PA waveform appears during systole	
Continuous wedge	PAWP waveform when monitoring PA	Catheter tip has spontaneously wedged (distinguish from a damped waveform)

PAP

Taking Pressure Readings from Waveforms

Readings of PASP, PAMP, PADP and PAWP should be taken at end-expiration (see Pgs. 7-24, 27).

Identifying end-expiration during PPV control or CPAP is fairly easy. In other modes, where there is a combination of spontaneous and mechanical breaths, it is more difficult and unpredictable.

Careful attention must be placed on the patient's breathing pattern. Other means of identifying end-expiration is by watching patient's chest, ventilator manometer (proximal airway pressures), respiratory waveform, and/or expiratory flow recordings.

Also, the patient should be calm, not moving, agitated, dyspneic, or "fighting" the ventilator.

Transmural pressures may be desired (see Pg. 7-36).

PWP Waveform Variations

Variation	Description	Cause
Respiratory: ①		
Spontaneous inspiration	↓ baseline pressure	normal
Spontaneous expiration	↑ baseline pressure	normal

```
10
mmHg
0        I              I
```

Positive Pressure Ventilation: ②		
Inspiration	↑ baseline pressure	Positive pressure ventilation, exaggerated with PEEP.
Expiration	↓ baseline pressure	Positive pressure ventilation, exaggerated with PEEP.

```
        E              E
```

① The extent of fluctuations is directly proportional to the extent of airway pressure changes. Often up to 10-20 mmHg.
② Pressure fluctuations are dependent on the mode of ventilation (ie: whether the ventilator or patient does most of the work.) (See also Pgs. 7-31 - 36)
③ Point of end-expiration, lowest proximal airway pressure and point of end expiratory flow. (See Pg. 7-26)

Variation	Description	Pathological Cause
Prominent a wave (exaggerated)	Exaggerated a wave (Canon wave)	↑ LA contraction: Mitral stenosis ↑ Resistance to LV filling: Mitral stenosis Aortic valve stenosis LVF LA contraction against a closed mitral valve: a-v dissociation 3° heart block
Absent a wave	No a wave present	↓ or absent atrial contraction Atrial fibrillation Junctional arrhythmias Ventricular pacing

PAP

7-27

Variation	Description	Pathological Cause
Prominent v wave 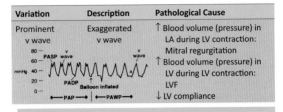	Exaggerated v wave	↑ Blood volume (pressure) in LA during LV contraction: Mitral regurgitation ↑ Blood volume (pressure) in LV during LV contraction: LVF ↓ LV compliance

Clinical Note: Giant v waves may be transmitted back onto the PAP waveform, producing a bifid wave (v wave may be ≥ PASP).
Caution: A prominent v wave may cause the PAWP waveform to resemble the PAP waveform. One may think the balloon is deflated when it is not! (To confirm location, see Pg. 7-11).

Variation	Description	Pathological Causes
Prominent a and v waves 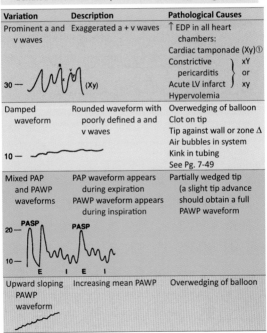	Exaggerated a + v waves	↑ EDP in all heart chambers: Cardiac tamponade (Xy)① Constrictive pericarditis } xY or Acute LV infarct } xy Hypervolemia
Damped waveform	Rounded waveform with poorly defined a and v waves	Overwedging of balloon Clot on tip Tip against wall or zone Δ Air bubbles in system Kink in tubing See Pg. 7-49
Mixed PAP and PAWP waveforms	PAP waveform appears during expiration PAWP waveform appears during inspiration	Partially wedged tip (a slight tip advance should obtain a full PAWP waveform
Upward sloping PAWP waveform	Increasing mean PAWP	Overwedging of balloon

① Xy = predominent X descent with a short or absent y descent.
xY = predominent Y descent.   xy = x and y descents are equal.

CLINICAL PROBLEMS IN OBTAINING ACCURATE PA CATHETER MEASUREMENTS

Problem	Clinical Note
Body position	Keep transducer's air-fluid interface level with phlebostatic axis (see Pg. 6-16). Keep measurement position as consistent as possible — Supine position is preferred (not necessary if patient cannot tolerate). Head up 0-20° is acceptable without significantly affecting PAP or PAWP values. Head up > 20° may produce inaccuracies, but acceptable for monitoring trends rather than absolutes.
Cardiac dysfunction	PAWP ≠ LAP ≠ LVEDP when some elements of cardiac dysfunction are present (see Pg. 7-20).
Catheter whip (Fling)	Excessive movement of catheter tip, seen as an artifact spike superimposed on a PAP waveform. PA pressures become unreliable (may observe trends, if whip cannot be eliminated). Causes: Catheter tip near pulmonic valve. Excessive catheter length. External noise (shivering or precordial movement). Hyperdynamic heart — Early sepsis Excessive cathecholamines
Catheter tip position (see Fig. overleaf)	PAP's increase progressively towards the lung bottom. (Tip position may be determined by a cross table lateral chest X-ray.)

PAP

Problem	Clinical Note
Zone 1	$P_A > P_a > P_v$ Vascular channel is continually closed, hence no patent vessel to LA. (PAWP ≠ LAP) PAWP ≈ PA (Wedged waveform appears damped.)
Zone 2	$P_a > P_A > P_v$ Vascular channel becomes closed during expiration. (PAWP ≈ LAP during inspiration.) (PAWP ≠ LAP during expiration.) PAWP ≈ PA (Wedged waveform appears damped)
Zone 3	$P_a > P_v > P_A$ Vascular channel is continually open. (PAWP ≈ LAP) PAWP ≈ Pv ≈ LAP (Wedged waveform should show LA a & v waves)

Note: When supine, the majority of the lung is Zone 3.

The size of Zone 1 and Zone 2 enlarges (moves downward with):

1) ↑ PA from PPV especially with PEEP or air-trapping (asthma, COPD) (see Pgs. 7-30 - 37)
2) ↓ Pa and ↓ Pv with hypovolemia, hemorrhage or diuresis.

Zone Placement Check

Test	Zone 1 or 2	Zone 3
PADP vs. PAWP	PADP < PAWP	PADP > PAWP
Respiratory variation	> 1/2 change in PAWP	< 1/2 change in PAWP
PAWP contour	damped, smooth contour	a, c & v waves
Catheter tip on x-ray	at or above LA	below LA
Δ PEEP trial	Δ PAWP > 1/2 Δ PEEP	Δ PAWP < 1/2 Δ PEEP

Zone 1

Intermittent flow Zone 2

Constant flow Zone 3

Problem	Clinical Note
Ventilatory effects: Spontaneous breathing	<u>Normal, quiet:</u> PAWP is minimally affected as intrathoracic pressure changes are transmitted to intravascular pressure changes. Inspiration → slight ↓PAWP Expiration → slight ↑ PAWP <u>Labored:</u> PAP and PAWP are greatly affected. Inspiration → large ↓ PAWP Expiration → large ↑ PAWP **Note:** Digital monitors may record PAWP highs and lows as PASP and PADP which will give inaccurate and inconsistent measurements. To improve accuracy: Have patient stop breathing momentarily at end expiration. If unable, read PAP and PAWP on portion of waveform corresponding to end expiration.

Problem	Clinical Note
Ventilatory effects, cont. Mechanical ventilation	Three different physiological effects are created.[1]
	Positive pressure ventilation, during inspiration, causes:
	1) ↑ PAWP ($\uparrow$ Pa → $\uparrow$ PIT → $\uparrow$ PIV → $\uparrow$ PAP → $\uparrow$ PAWP) Measure PAWP at end expiration.
	2) ↓ CO ($\uparrow$ PA → $\uparrow$ PIT → ↓ venous return → ↓ CO)
	3) ↑ Zone 1 and 2 ($\uparrow$ Pa > Pa and/or Pv) (see Pg. 7-30).
Mechanical ventilation with PEEP	PEEP exaggerates the effects described above under mechanical ventilation.
	PEEP 0–10cmH$_2$O → PAWP ≈ LAP and LVEDP
	PEEP > 10cmH$_2$O → increasing disparity between PAWP and LH pressures
	Estimating PEEP effects (see Pg. 7-35)

[1] ↓ Lung compliance → ↓ transmission of pressures → ↓ effects
↑ Lung compliance → ↑ transmission of pressures → ↑ effects

OVERVIEW OF VENTILATORY EFFECTS ON HEMODYNAMIC PRESSURES

NORMAL SPONTANEOUS BREATHING

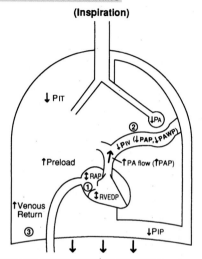

(Inspiration)

① Preload:
$$\downarrow \text{diaphragm} \rightarrow \downarrow P_{IT} \rightarrow \downarrow P_{IC} \rightarrow \downarrow RAP + \downarrow RVEDP$$
$$\downarrow P_{IT} \rightarrow \uparrow \text{venous return} \longrightarrow \uparrow RAP + \uparrow RVEDP$$
$\left.\begin{array}{c} \\ \\ \end{array}\right\}$ $\downarrow$ RAP usually dominates

② RV Afterload:
$$\downarrow P_{IT} \rightarrow \downarrow P_{IV} \longrightarrow \downarrow PAP$$
$$\uparrow \text{venous return} \rightarrow$$
$$\uparrow RVEDP \rightarrow \uparrow PA \text{ flow} \longrightarrow \uparrow PAP$$
$\left.\begin{array}{c} \\ \\ \end{array}\right\}$ $\downarrow$ PAP usually dominates

③ The lungs act as a circulatory assist pump during inspiration.

Expiration → reverse of inspiration.

Summary

Hemodynamic parameters are minimally affected by normal spontaneous breathing. Measurements should be made at end-expiration, when pressure changes are at a minimal. (Have patient hold breath if possible. Watch for inadvertant Valsalva.)

During labored breathing the above effects are increased.

POSITIVE PRESSURE VENTILATION

Inspiration

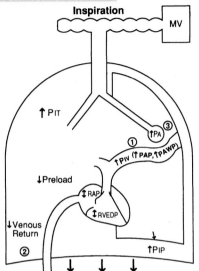

① RV Afterload:
$\uparrow$ Pa $\rightarrow$ $\uparrow$ Pit $\rightarrow$ $\uparrow$ Piv ($\uparrow$ PAP, $\uparrow$ PAWP) $\rightarrow$ $\uparrow$ PVR $\rightarrow$
$\uparrow$ RV afterload $\rightarrow$ $\downarrow$ PA flow $\rightarrow$ $\downarrow$ LA filling $\rightarrow$ $\downarrow$ LAP $\rightarrow$ $\downarrow$ CO

② Preload:
$\uparrow$ Pit $\rightarrow$ $\downarrow$ venous return $\rightarrow$ $\downarrow$ RAP
(possible $\downarrow$ CO + $\downarrow$ PA flow) } $\uparrow$ RAP usually dominates
$\uparrow$ Pa $\rightarrow$ $\uparrow$ Pit $\rightarrow$ $\uparrow$ Pic $\rightarrow$ $\uparrow$ RAP

③ $\uparrow$ Pa $\rightarrow$ enlarges zone 1 & 2. If PA cath tip in a zone 1 or 2, then
PAWP may reflect Pa .

Note:

MV & PEEP $\rightarrow$ $\uparrow$ Pit $\rightarrow$ $\downarrow$ LV afterload

Hence acts as a LV assist in patients with LV dysfunction.
Weaning PEEP or PPV, therefore, will $\uparrow$ LV afterload and
$\downarrow$ LV assist and possibly precipitate acute LV failure and
pulmonary edema.

Expiration $\rightarrow$ reverse of inspiration   Summary: Next page

Summary:

Cardiovascular effects of positive pressure ventilation are directly proportional to the $\uparrow$ PIT (ie: level and mode of ventilation and lung compliance).

> **Note:** Patients with pre-existing depressed cardiac function or hypovolemia are more susceptible to the pressure changes.

Hemodynamic measurements, therefore, should be made at end-expiration, when pressure changes are minimal. (Delay onset of inspiration if possible.

PEEP

PEEP (including auto-PEEP) exaggerates the effects of PPV during inspiration and maintains some of those effects during expiration (ie: continuous $\uparrow$ PIT).

> **Note:** Exaggeration is greatest in lungs with increased compliance.
> PEEP, however, is most commonly used in patients with $\downarrow$ lung compliance.
> PEEP effects become less well transmitted to pulmonary vasculature as lung compliance decreases.

Estimating "true" hemodynamic values while on PEEP

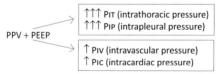

$$\text{PPV + PEEP} \quad \longrightarrow \quad \boxed{\begin{array}{l} \uparrow\uparrow\uparrow \text{ PIT (intrathoracic pressure)} \\ \uparrow\uparrow\uparrow \text{ PIP (intrapleural pressure)} \end{array}}$$
$$\longrightarrow \quad \boxed{\begin{array}{l} \uparrow \text{ PIV (intravascular pressure)} \\ \uparrow \text{ PIC (intracardiac pressure)} \end{array}}$$

PPV and PEEP increase intrathoracic pressure (PIT) or intrapleural pressure (PIP) more than they increase intravascular (PIV) or intracardiac (PIC) pressures.

PIV and PIC are commonly referenced to atmospheric pressure, but when PIT is increased, they should be referenced to transmural pressure (PTM).

PIT or PIP = is normally ignored due to small value (–3 mmHg), but should be subtracted from obtained value when significant.
Can be measured by esophageal catheter or estimated. **7-35**

Transmural Pressure (Ptm):

$$
\begin{aligned}
\text{PTM} &= \text{"true" pressure} \\
&= \text{P measure} \quad - \quad \text{intrathoracic pressure} \\
&= \text{PIV} \quad\quad\quad - \quad \text{PIT} \\
&\quad\ (\text{or PIC}) \\
&= \text{PAWP} \quad\ - \quad \text{PIP} \\
&\quad\ (\text{CVP, etc.})
\end{aligned}
$$

Measuring PIP — insert esophageal balloon (rarely done clinically)

Estimating PIP —
1) $\text{PIP} \approx \text{PA}$ (alveolar pressure)
2) $\text{PIP} \approx \% \text{PEEP}$

Note —

1) $\text{PA} \approx$ to plateau pressure on ventilator manometer at end expiration when exhalation port is occluded. This relationship is not always accurate, especially when forced exhalations or air-trapping is present. Respiratory muscle paralysis may be used to eliminate the respiratory fluctuations.

2) In compliant lungs: $\text{PIP} \approx 1/2\ \text{PEEP}$
   In non-compliant lungs: $\text{PIP} \approx 0\ \text{to}\ 1/3\ \text{PEEP}$

Examples

1) Normal spontaneous breathing:

$$
\begin{aligned}
\text{True PAWP} &= \text{PAWP} \quad - \quad \text{PIP} \\
&= 15\ \text{mmHg} \quad - \quad (-3\ \text{mmHg}) \\
&= 18\ \text{mmHg}
\end{aligned}
$$

2) Mechanical ventilation with 15 cmH$_2$O PEEP

$$
\begin{aligned}
\text{True PAWP} &= \text{PAWP} \quad - \quad \text{PIP} \\
&= \text{PAWP} \quad - \quad 1/2\ \text{PEEP} \\
&= 15\ \text{mmHg} \quad - \quad 1/2\ (15\ \text{cm H}_2\text{O}) \\
&= 15\ \text{mmHg} \quad - \quad 1/2\ (10\ \text{mmHg}) \\
&= 15\ \text{mmHg} \quad - \quad 5\ \text{mmHg} \\
&= 10\ \text{mmHg}
\end{aligned}
$$

Summary: Measured PAWP is almost always an overestimation of true PAWP when on PPV and PEEP.

PAWP— $\uparrow$ PEEP $\rightarrow$ $\uparrow$ P$_{IT}$ $\rightarrow$ $\uparrow$ P$_{IV}$ $\rightarrow$ $\uparrow$ PAWP

Plus as PEEP levels increase, the size of zones 1 & 2 increase and the size of zone 3 decreases:

PEEP 0-10 usually not much zone change;

PEEP > 10, zone change increases proportionately.

Zone 1 $\rightarrow$	PAWP ≈ P$_A$	
Zone 2 $\rightarrow$	Inspiration:	PAWP ≈ P$_A$
	Expiration:	PAWP ≈ LAP
Zone 3 $\rightarrow$	PAWP ≈ LAP	

As the zones change when PEEP is added, the PA catheter tip location may go from being in a zone 3 to a zone 2 or 1.

Zone 3 to Zone 2

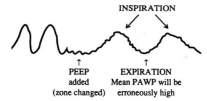

INSPIRATION

$\uparrow$
PEEP
added
(zone changed)

$\uparrow$
EXPIRATION
Mean PAWP will be
erroneously high

Zone 3 to Zone 1

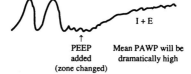

I + E

$\uparrow$
PEEP
added
(zone changed)

Mean PAWP will be
dramatically high

Note: If PAWP increases > 1/2 the added PEEP, then tip may be in Zone 1 or 2 (see Pg. 7-30).

Although PPV and PEEP results in $\uparrow$ PAWP values, most clinicians keep the patient on the machine and measure the results at end expiration.

Advantage of leaving patient on PPV and PEEP:

Primary interest is the patient's hemodynamic state *during* PPV and PEEP support.

Disadvantages of removing patient from PPV and PEEP:

Measurements will only reflect the <u>temporary</u> hemodynamic state during removal.

Disconnection will result in —

1) Sudden changes in hemodynamic state:
   Sudden $\uparrow$ venous return $\rightarrow$ $\uparrow$ RA blood $\rightarrow$ $\uparrow$ LA blood
   Sudden release of compression on pulmonary
      capillaries $\rightarrow$ $\uparrow$ LA blood
   Sudden change in ventricular diastolic dynamics

2) Loss of alveolar stability and small airway collapse:
   Sudden $\downarrow$ PaO_2
   Sudden change in FRC

3) Loss of airway pressure:
   Potential alveolar flooding

4) Sudden change in $\dot{V}/\dot{Q}$
   $\uparrow$ intrapulmonary shunting
   change in PVR

5) These changes are not immediately reestablished when patient is placed back on positive pressure.

Complication	Causes	Preventive Care / Treatment / Clinical Notes
Insertion		
Trauma: Pneumothorax	Pleural puncture by needle	Needle insertion must be done cautiously and skillfully. Right side preferred (lung and pleura are lower) Insert chest tube as needed.
Puncture/rupture of: vessel heart wall heart valve pulmonary artery	Perforation of conduit channel by needle or catheter	Needle insertion must be done cautiously and skillfully. Catheter should be advanced slowly, without force. Fluoroscopy may be required if difficult to pass.
Knotting/looping of catheter	Repeated advances and withdrawals during insertion. Dilated cardiac chambers Excessively long catheter	Undo knot/loop via fluoroscope observation. (Insure balloon deflated upon withdrawal) Surgical removal may be necessary. If knot or loop goes undetected or occurs following insertion, resistance will be felt upon removal. Do not pull against resistance! Confirm with CXR.
Catheter		
Arrhythmia Tachyarrhythmia	Irritation of endocardium by the catheter with: Insertion	Keep balloon inflated during advancement.

PAP

Complication	Causes	Preventive Care / Treatment / Clinical Notes
Catheter, cont.		
	Backward slippage	Usually when tip migrates from PA back into RV. (Confirm with CXR and inflate balloon to float tip back into PA.)
	↑ Risk factors	Correct risk factors if possible: Acidosis Ischemia/infarct Digitalis toxicity Shock Hypoxemia Ventricular failure Electrolyte imbalance (Ca^{++}, K^{+}, Mg^{++})
Bradyarrhythmia	Irritation of Bundle of His in patients with left bundle branch block	Treat with antiarrhythmic drugs. Defibrillate if necessary. Be prepared to provide internal or external pacing if a RBBB complicates an antecedent LBBB.
Balloon rupture	Overinflation Removal of air with negative pressure Inflation with fluid Excessive number of inflations Defective balloon	Clinical indications of balloon rupture: Blood in balloon lumen Failure to wedge Lack of resistance during inflation No air back when pressure on syringe is released PA waveform persists after inflation

Complication	Causes	Preventive Care / Treatment / Clinical Notes
Catheter, cont.		**Confirmation of balloon rupture:** Inflate balloon using a glass syringe. The barrel will spring back when released, if the balloon is intact. **Caution:** Do not test for balloon rupture with air more than once. Use CO_2 to test for rupture if patient is suspected of having a R-L shunt. Treatment: (see Pg. 7-13 also) Catheter does not have to be removed. Label catheter port and notify personnel so no further wedge attempts will be made. Use PADP, if possible, to assess PAWP, LAP, LVEDP, and LV function (see Pg. 7-19, 20). Replace catheter if necessary.
Electric microshock	Improper electric precaution	Observe electrical saftey guidelines. Currents < 1 amp may travel via this route.
Embolism: Air	Air entry from: Insertion Tubing changes Blood sampling Giving meds	Keep system free of air and connections tight. Remove any air that enters system. Keep patient flat when opening a subclavian or jugular system and have patient hold breath at end expiration.
	Balloon rupture	See previous page and Pg. 7-13

PAP

7-41

Complication	Causes	Preventive Care / Treatment / Clinical Notes
Catheter, cont.		
Thrombus	Blood clot from: Catheter tip Catheter kink Poor fluid flow Vessel trauma	Insure steady flow of heparinized infusate. Always aspirate first, before flushing. **Note:** If aspiration fails to produce a blood return — do not flush. Remove catheter.
	Balloon fragments from rupture	Increased risk in patients with hypercoaguable states: cancer, fever, MI, polycythemia Avoid vigorous flushing and do not flush in PAWP position. Cerebral and/or systemic embolization is possible if R-L shunt is present. Clinical indication of clot: 1) Damped pressure 2) ↑ PASP, ↑ PADP, and ↑ PADP - PAWP gradient 3) Poor IV infusion or flush
Infection	Break in sterile technique during insertion	Insure sterile technique
	Catheter contamination	See infection control (Pg. 5-18). Once catheter in place, do not push further in. Use aseptic/sterile technique during dressing changes. Remove/replace catheter ASAP or after 72-96 hrs.

Complication	Causes	Preventive Care / Treatment / Clinical Notes

Catheter, cont.	Contaminated IV fluid	Change IV solution, tubing, stopcock, and transducers q 48 hrs.
		Do not use IV fluid containing glucose.
		Check disposable transducer domes for cracks and replace after countershock.
		Signs and symptoms of infection — see Pg. 5-18.
		
		Incidence of infection is directly proportional to:
		  1) Length of time catheter is in place.
		  2) Number of manipulations (blood withdrawals, IV push meds, CO studies, repositioning).

Pulmonary artery rupture	Balloon overinflation	Treatment: Remove catheter and institute antibiotic therapy. Never inject more than recommended volume.
	Spontaneous migration of tip into small vessel	Inject air slowly and *only* enough to obtain a PAWP waveform. (Obtain periodic X-ray to confirm tip location.)
	Flotation of catheter with less than recommended volume	Never advance catheter with less than recommended volume.

Complication	Causes	Preventive Care / Treatment / Clinical Notes
Catheter, cont.		
Pulmonary artery rupture, cont.	Flushing of a wedged catheter	Never flush in the wedged position (insure balloon is deflated).

	Forced irrigation	Never force irrigation.
		
		Note: Increased incidence in patients with:
		  Anticoagulable states
		  Cardiopulmonary bypass surgery
		  Old age (> 60)
		  Pulmonary hypertension
		
		Clinical evidence for a ruptured artery:
		  1) Aspiration of air through the distal lumen.
		  2) Hemoptysis

Complication	Causes	Preventive Care / Treatment / Clinical Notes
Catheter, cont.		
Pulmonary artery rupture, cont.		Treatment: If hemoptysis is small, place patient in lateral recumbent position, affected side down, and monitor closely. If massive hemoptysis (> 15ml) occurs, place patient with affected side down. Intubate and ventilate if needed (may need double lumen ET tube). Remove or reposition catheter. Surgical repair if needed.
Pulmonary infarct or ischemia	Prolonged wedging (from balloon inflation)	Insure inflation time < 15 secs. Insure PA waveform returns following deflation.
	Persistent wedging (from spontaneous migration)	Noted by a PAWP waveform without balloon inflation.
	Embolization of a thrombus	See Pg. 7-42 and 10-33.
		Insure continuous monitoring.

A General Systematic Approach
(See next page for specific troubleshooting.)

1. <u>Check patient:</u> Assess for physiological changes such as evidence of shock or hemodynamic changes.

2. <u>Check proximal to catheter:</u>
   A. Pressure bag — check for adequate pressure.
   B. Transducer dome — check for air, looseness or cracks.
   C. Transducer level — check level with phlebostatic axis (see Page 6-16.)
   D. Tubing — check: stopcock positions, connections for looseness, kinks, air or blood.

   > Note: If air or blood in tubing —
   > 1. Gently aspirate with syringe until pulmonary artery blood appears. (Do not aspirate if tip is suspected of being wedged.)
   > 2. Gently flush with irrigating solution.

3. <u>Check monitoring system:</u> check zero and calibration, amplifier setting, etc.

4. <u>Check catheter:</u>

   Patency — Gently aspirate and flush.
   If unable to aspirate or flush gently, tip or lumen is probably fully clotted. Do not force flush.
   Replace catheter.

   Balloon — See Pgs. 7-13 and 7-40.

   Position — If catheter tip is suspected of being against a wall, turn patient side to side and have them cough.

   If catheter tip is suspected of spontaneous wedging, obtain an X-ray to verify. Withdraw catheter carefully until proper waveforms appear.

PAP

Troubleshooting the PA Line (Specifics)		
Problem	**Possible Causes**	**Prevention/Correction**
Sudden pressure change	Air bubbles or clot	Aspirate (see Pg. 7-42)
	Catheter tip position changed	Check position with X-ray or fluoroscopy
	Transducer level or patient position changed	Check and correct level of transducer with phlebostatic axis (see Pg. 6-16)
	Incorrect zero or calibration	Check and/or recalibrate (see Pg. 5-12)
No waveform	Amplifier off or on zero	Check and correct
	Cable disconnected	Connect cable
	Complete occlusion with clot	Aspirate if possible (see Pg. 7-42) (Do not flush if cannot aspirate) Change catheter if necessary
	Loose connection	A large leak should be apparent with blood backing up catheter
	Stopcock in wrong position	Check and correct
	Transducer connected to wrong monitor outlet	Check and correct
	Transducer defective	Replace transducer
	Transducer dome is broken, cracked, loose or large air bubble	Check, correct or replace

PAP

Problem	Possible Causes	Prevention/Correction
All waveforms damped	Air bubble present	Aspirate bubble
	Flush bag not fully inflated	Check and pressurize to 300 mmHg
	Incorrect calibration	Calibrate and zero
Damped RA waveform	Stopcock position partly closed	Adjust
	Partial clot	Aspirate clot (see Pg. 7-42).
Damped PA waveform	Air bubble in line	Aspirate bubble
	Amplifier setting incorrect	Check and correct
	Balloon overinflated	Check balloon inflation
	Catheter or tubing kinked.	Check and correct Check for internal kink or coil with x-ray
	Catheter tip advanced to wedge or near-wedge position	Deflate balloon. Change patient position and/or cough Reposition catheter if necessary
	Catheter tip against wall	Change patient position and/or cough Reposition catheter if necessary
	Incorrect stopcock position	Check and correct
	Incorrect zero and/or calibration	Check and correct
	Loose line connection with leak in system	Check setup and insure tight connections
	Partial clot in line	Aspirate clot (see Pg. 7-42).

Problem	Possible Causes	Prevention/Correction
Damped PA waveform, cont.	Patient's condition Transducer or dome faulty.	Check for shock Check and correct
Damped PAWP waveform	Overinflation of balloon Tip in Zone 1 or 2 See also Pg. 7-28	Inject only enough to obtain PAWP waveform See Pg. 7-30
PAWP waveform obtained with less than recommended volume	Catheter advanced too far or spontaneous migration of tip	Change patient position and/or cough Check catheter tip with X-ray or fluoroscopy Reposition catheter if necessary
Spontaneous and/or continuous PAWP waveform	Balloon inflated Catheter advanced too far or spontaneous migration of tip	Deflate balloon Change patient position and/or cough Check catheter tip with X-ray or fluoroscopy Reposition catheter if necessary
Unable to obtain PAWP waveform (PA waveform is normal)	Balloon rupture Catheter tip not advanced far enough Insufficient balloon inflation	See Pg. 7-40. Clamp balloon port, label and notify physician Document with X-ray Reposition patient or catheter (Do not overfill balloon) Deflate balloon and reinflate with exact amount

Problem	Possible Causes	Prevention/Correction
RV waveform present:		
Distal port	Catheter tip has slipped backwards into RV.	Reposition catheter.
Proximal port	Catheter is too far advanced.	Reposition catheter.
Artifact, noise or fling	Catheter whip	Avoid excessive catheter length. Try different tip position.
	Electrical interference	Have biomedical department check.
	Patient movement	Limit patient movement.
Bleeding:		
Catheter or tubing	Leak in system	Check and tighten all connections.
Insertion site	Trauma or improperly stabilized	Apply local pressure until bleeding stops. Stabilize catheter
Catheter accidentally removed	Accidental	Apply local pressure until bleeding stops. Notify physician
Fluctuations	Heart beat	Abnormal — tip has slipped back into RV
	Respirations	Normal.
	Positive pressure ventilation	Insure readings are taken in a consistent manner (end expiration)

Problem	Possible Causes	Prevention/Correction
IV infusion slowed or stopped	Blood clot	Aspirate then flush Insure continuous heparinized infusion.
	Kink in tubing or catheter.	Check and correct.
	Catheter tip against vessel wall or wedged	Change patient position and/or cough.
	Loss of adequate pressure in bag.	Insure adequate pressure.
	Stopcock in wrong position.	Check and correct.

PAP

General guidelines only. Follow hospital protocol. Removal
guidelines are basically the same for different sites.

PAP

General —

PA catheters should be removed ASAP. (They should not be left
in place as a CVP monitoring line or as a venous line.)

Removal should be performed by or under the supervision of an
experienced physician.

Strict aseptic technique is required.

Know and understand correct procedure. (Be aware of
complications.)

Explain procedure to patient.

Monitor vital signs and EKG during and after removal. Watch for
ventricular arrhythmias.

Have crash cart and defibrillator on standby.

Never force the withdrawal if resistance is met.

Obtain chest X-ray following removal.

Equipment —

Sterile: gauze sponges, gloves, iodophor ointment, nonallergenic
tape, suture removal kit, towels or drapes.

Procedure —

1. Position patient supine (or no more than 30° to 45° head
   elevation if other than jugular or subclavian).
2. Insure all air is removed from balloon.
3. Turn off flush solutions.
4. Remove dressing and sutures.
5. Carefully withdraw catheter.
   Watch VS and EKG.
   Watch for kinks or loops.
   Never force withdrawal if resistance is met.
6. Immediately apply direct pressure at insertion site with
   a sterile pad for 5-10 minutes or until bleeding stops.
   (Increase holding time for patients with increased bleeding
   tendency.)
7. Clean site, apply iodophor and sterile pressure dressing.
8. Remove sterile dressing after 10 minutes and assess site
   (a sandbag is often placed on a femoral site and left for
   two hours.)

9. If bleeding persists, reapply pressure for another 5-10 minutes. Notify physician if further complications.
10. Clean site, apply iodophor ointment and cover with sterile dressing.
11. Recheck site after 1 hour and 4 hours.
12. Document removal and patient assessment.
13. Obtain chest X-ray.

PAP

8   Cardiac Output Monitoring

Cardiac Output

Cardiac Output Monitoring Overview

Non-Invasive Cardiac Monitoring*

Echocardiography
  Transesophageal Echocardiography (TEE)
Impedance Cardiography (ICG)
  Electrical Impedance Plethysmography (EIP)
  Thoracic Electrical Bioimpedance (TEB)
  TEB & BioReactance™ (NICOM™)
  ICG & IPG (niccomo™)

Minimally Invasive Cardiac Monitoring*

Esophageal Doppler Ultrasonography
Lithium Dilution (LiDCO™)
Partial CO2 Rebreathing (NICO™)
Pulse Contour Analysis with Thermodilution
  (PiCCO™)
Pulse Dye Densitometry
Pulse Power Analysis (LiDCO™ *plus*)
Transpulmonary Thermodilution (arterial)

*All of these are newer techniques are still being studied and beyond the scope of this book at this time.

Invasive Cardiac Monitoring

See following pages:

HEMODYNAMIC PARAMETERS DERIVED FROM CO MEASUREMENT

Parameter	Definition	Equation	Normals	Clinical Note
Cardiac Index (CI)	Cardiac output per body surface area	CI = CO/BSA	2.5-4.0 L/min/m²	CI = 1.8-2.2 indicates hypoperfusion. CI < 1.8 indicates shock. To find BSA — see Appendix
Cardiac Output (CO)	Amount of blood pumped by the heart per minute	CO = HR × SV	4-8 L/min	See Pg. 2-20.
Ejection Fraction (EF)	Percentage of ventricular chamber emptying (amount of blood ejected per total volume)	EF = SV/EDV	65% (50-75%)	Measured by ventriculogram, nuclear imaging, or echo. See Pg. 2-26.
Stroke Volume (SV)	Amount of blood ejected per ventricle per contraction	SV = CO/HR SV = EDV-ESV	60-120 ml/beat	See Pg. 2-26.
Stroke Volume Index (SVI)	Stroke volume per body surface area	SVI = SV/BSA	35-75 ml/m²/beat	To find BSA, see Appendix
Stroke Work (SW)	Measure of ventricle performance (how hard it works to eject blood)	SW = SV × V press	60-80 g/m/beat (LV)	See Pgs. 1-13 and 2-26.

Cardiac Output

Cardiac Output

Parameter	Definition	Equation	Normals	Clinical Note
Stroke Work Index (SWI)	Measure of ventricle performance per body surface area	$SWI = SW/BSA$	40–75 gm/m/beat/m^2	See Appendix for BSA
Systemic Vascular Resistance (SVR)	Resistance to LV ejection of blood into systemic circulation	$SVR = \dfrac{(BP-RAP) \times 80}{CO}$	1200–1600 dynes•sec•cm^{-5}	See Pg. 2-39. SVR is a measure of work imposed on the Ⓛ heart.
Systemic Vascular Resistance Index (SVRI)	Resistance to LV ejection of blood into systemic circulation per body surface area	$SVRI = SVR/BSA$ $SVRI = \dfrac{(BP-RAP) \times 80}{CI}$	250–650 dynes•sec•cm^{-5}/m^2	See Appendix for BSA
Pulmonary Vascular Resistance (PVR)	Resistance to RV ejection of blood into pulmonary vasculature	$PVR = \dfrac{(PAP-PAWP) \times 80}{CO}$	20–250 dynes•sec•cm^{-5}	See Pg. 2-44. PVR is a measure of work imposed on the Ⓡ heart.
Pulmonary Vascular Resistance Index (PVRI)	Resistance to RV ejection of blood into pulmonary vasculature per body surface area	$PVRI = PVR/BSA$ $PVRI = \dfrac{(PAP-PAWP) \times 80}{CI}$	200–280 dynes•sec•cm^{-5}/m^2	See Appendix for BSA

INVASIVE METHODS OF CO MEASUREMENT — AN OVERVIEW

Method	Requirements	Advantages	Disadvantages	Clinical Notes
Fick	Simultaneous collection of: ① PIO$_2$ (O$_2$ analyzer) PaO$_2$ & PaCO$_2$ (ABG) PvO$_2$ + PvCO$_2$ (PA cath) PEO$_2$ (collection system)	Extremely accurate even in patients with ↓CO, intracardiac shunts or valvular insufficiency. Indicates status of pulmonary system.	No practical clinical application, time-consuming and technically complex. Patient must remain in steady state (no change due to pain, anxiety, shivering, etc.) during entire procedure. Requires at least 2 people for the procedure. Both arterial and venous blood and patient cooperation is needed. Affected by O$_2$ administration. High chance of error.	Commonly done in cath lab, rarely done at bedside. Concept: See page 8-7

① SaO$_2$ and SvO$_2$ may be used instead of blood sampling.

Cardiac Output

Method	Requirements	Advantages	Disadvantages	Clinical Notes
Indicator (dye) dilution (see pg 8-9)	A-line, PA catheter and computer	Accurate ±5%. Faster and easier than Fick. Not affected by O_2 administration.	Precision requirements make this impractical for bedside. Less accurate than Fick in presence of ↓CO, intracardiac shunts or valvular insufficiency. Requires arterial and venous blood. Patient may have adverse reaction to dye.	Used only in research
Thermodilution (see pg 8-9)	Thermodilution PA catheter Computer	Performed by one person. Only one catheter is needed. No blood withdrawal. Rapid, simple and easy. Good reproducibility. Not affected by O_2 administration.	Not accurate with ↓CO, intracardiac shunt or valvular insufficiency. Potential fluid overload if frequent measurements made. May cause arrhythmias, esp. if iced injectate.	Most commonly used invasive bedside determination of CO. Considered the "gold standard"

Concept

$$CO = \frac{O_2 \text{ consumption}}{\text{arterio-venous } O_2 \text{ content difference}}$$

$$= \frac{\dot{V}O_2}{Ca - \bar{v}O_2} \text{ ①}$$

O_2 consumption = O_2 content of inspired gas – O_2 content of expired gas.

= O_2 removed by cells.

(O_2 removed by cells = O_2 removed from inspired air.)

Example: $CO = \dfrac{250 \text{ ml/min}}{20 \text{ vol \%} - 15 \text{ vol \%}} = \dfrac{250 \text{ ml/min}}{5\%}$
$= \dfrac{250}{0.05} = 5000 \text{ ml/min} = 5 \text{ l/m}$
Normal O_2 consumption range = 180-290 ml/min.
Normal $Ca-\bar{v}O_2$ range = 3–5.5 vol % (> 5.5 = ↓ CO).

Technique — (beyond the scope of this text)

Estimated CO by Fick

Note: Direct measurement of O_2 consumption is sometimes not available. O_2 consumption is, therefore, often estimated.

Normal O_2 consumption is 125ml O_2/min/m², (range 110-150) in a basal metabolic state. The greater the variation from a basal state, the less accurate the estimate (see below).

$$CO = \frac{125\text{ml } O_2/\text{min/m}^2 \times BSA}{Ca-\bar{v}O_2} \quad \text{or} \quad \frac{3.5 \times Wt \text{ (kg)}}{Ca-vO_2}$$

Variations in basal metabolic state		
↑ O_2 *consumption*		↓ O_2 *consumption*
activity	seizures	anesthesia
anxiety	shivering	hypothermia
hyperthermia	↑ WOB	induced paralysis
pain		sepsis (cold phase)
		↓ WOB (PPV)

① Fick Equation: $\dot{V}O_2 = CO \times Ca - \bar{v}O_2$

$Ca-\bar{v}O_2 = [(SaO_2 \times Hgb \times 1.36) + (PaO_2 \times 0.0031)] -$
$\quad [(SvO_2 \times Hgb \times 1.36) + (P\bar{v}O_2 \times 0.0031)]$

$Sa-\bar{v}O_2$ may be substituted for $Ca-\bar{v}O_2$: SaO_2 and $S\bar{v}O_2$
measurements may be used instead of blood sampling.

Dissolved O_2 ($PaO_2 + P\bar{v}O_2$) is clinically ignored. See also Pg. 2-7.

Indicator Dye Dilution Method

Concept — Measurement of the dilution of a dye, by blood, injected into the circulatory system

Indicator dye is injected into the pulmonary artery and peripheral arterial blood samples are withdrawn at set intervals. The density of the dye is measured spectro-photometrically, plotted, and CO is calculated by a computer.

Technique — A discussion of the technique is beyond the scope of this text.

Thermodilution Method

Concept — Measurement of the temperature change of blood following injection of a solution of a different temperature:

A specified quantity of saline or D5W at iced or room temperature is injected rapidly into the proximal (RA) port of a thermodilution PA catheter.

The temperature drop of blood is measured at the distal tip. The temperature change is plotted and CO is calculated by a computer.

Technique — Two techniques are currently employed:
Open Injectate Delivery System
Closed Injectate Delivery System (Preferred)

A discussion of the technique is beyond the scope of this text.

Newer catheters allow for continuous CO monitoring.

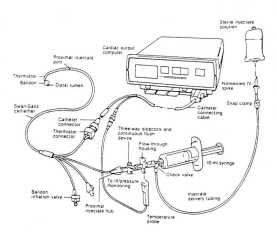

Reprinted with permission from *Critical Care Nursing: A Holistic Approach,* 5th Ed., Hudak, C. et al. Copyright 1990 by J.B. Lippincott Co., Philadelphia.

Interpretation of Thermodilution CO Curve

The normal curve should have:
    a smooth rapid upstroke (indicating rapid and even injection)
    an even downslope (indicating blood flow)

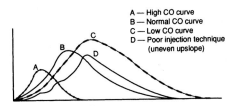

A — High CO curve
B — Normal CO curve
C — Low CO curve
D — Poor injection technique
    (uneven upslope)

Potential Sources of Error

Physiological causes:

Cardiac rate change, arrhythmias, altered hemodynamic status, or patient temperature change.

Mechanical ventilation — always inject at end expiration (PA blood temperature and CO varies during the ventilatory cycle).

Position change or movement of patient (change in venous return).

Intracardiac shunts or severe valve disease.

Technical causes:

Unequal amounts of injectate.

Slow or uneven injection of injectate.

Injectate temperature change —
    excessive handling
    tubing exposed to heat lamp, etc.

Improper positioning of thermistor head (too far advanced or in RH).

CLINICAL NOTE

CO readings may be correlated with $S\bar{v}O_2$ readings to check for discrepancies:

   $\downarrow$ CO with normal $S\bar{v}O_2$ = error in CO measurement.
   $\uparrow$ CO with low $S\bar{v}O_2$ = error in CO measurement.
   (Exceptions = sepsis or O_2 utilization disorders)

Cardiac Output

CAUSES OF DECREASED OR INCREASED CO

Event	Pathophysiology	Impact on hemodynamic function	Medical diagnosis
Decreased cardiac output	Acute heart muscle damage	Decreased contractility Increased preload Decreased or increased heart rate	Acute myocardial infarction
	Chronic heart muscle damage	Decreased contractility Increased preload Decreased or increased heart rate	Aortic or mitral valve disease Cardiomyopathy (dilated)
	Decreased venous return and compression of heart chambers	Decreased preload Decreased contractility Equalization of intracardiac pressures	Cardiac tamponade Trauma Aortic dissection into the pericardium After open heart surgery Effusion (pericardial) Cardiomyopathy (restrictive)
	Increased left-ventricular workload with increased systemic vascular resistance	Increased afterload	Hypothermia after cardiopulmonary bypass/open heart surgery Septic shock (late) Coarctation of the aorta
	Increased left-ventricular workload with normal systemic vascular resistance	Increased contractility Normal systemic vascular resistance	Aortic stenosis Cardiomyopathy (hypertrophic)
	Increased right-ventricular workload	Increased pulmonary vascular resistance	Idiopathic pulmonary hypertension Chronic obstructive pulmonary disease Congenital heart disease (with right-to-left shunt)

Cardiac Output

Event	Pathophysiology	Impact on hemodynamic function	Medical diagnosis
	Decreased circulating blood volume	Decreased preload Increased heart rate Increased afterload	Bleeding Traumatic injury After surgery Coagulopathy Internal bleeding (occult)
		Decreased heart rate	Bradycardia Three degree heart block Idioventricular rhythm Myocardial infarction
	Decreased diastolic filling time with decreased stroke volume	Increased heart rate Decreased preload	Tachycardia Paroxysmal atrial tachycardia Ventricular tachycardia
	Loss of heart rhythm	Cardiac arrest	Ventricular tachycardia Ventricular fibrillation Asystole
Increased cardiac output	Vasodilation	Decreased afterload Decreased preload Increased heart rate	Rewarming after open heart surgery Septic shock (early) Use of inotropic/vasodilator therapy

Reprinted with permission from Thelan, L. et al: *Textbook of Critical Care Nursing*. Copyright 1990 by C.V. Mosby Co., St. Louis.

Troubleshooting CO Measurements		
Problem	**Cause**	**Action**
Cardiac output values lower than expected	Injectate volume greater than designated amount	Inject exact volume to correspond to computation constant used.
	Catheter tip in RV or RA	Verify PA waveform from distal lumen. Reposition catheter.
	Incorrect computation constant (CC)	Reset computation constant. Correct prior CO values: Incorrect CO value × $\dfrac{\text{Correct CC}}{\text{Incorrect CC}}$ = Correct CC
	Left-to-right shunt (VSD)	Check RA & PA oxygen saturations. Use alternative CO measurement technique.
	Catheter kinked or partially obstructed with clot	Check for kinks at insertion site; straighten catheter; aspirate and flush catheter.
	Faulty catheter (communication between proximal and distal lumens)	Replace catheter.
Cardiac output values higher than expected	Injectate volume less than designated amount	Inject exact volume to correspond to computation constant. Carefully remove all air bubbles from syringe.
	Catheter too distal (PAW)	Verify PA waveform from distal lumen. Pull catheter back.
	RA port lies within sheath	Advance catheter.

Problem	Cause	Action
	Thermistor against wall of PA	Reposition patient. Rotate catheter to turn thermistor away from wall. Reposition catheter.
	Fibrin covering thermistor	Check a-vO_2 difference, change catheter.
	Incorrect computation constant (CC)	Correct prior CO values (see formula above). Reset computation constant.
	Right-to-left shunt (VSD)	Use alternative CO measurement technique.
	Incorrect injectate temperature	Use closed injectate system with in-line temperature probe. If syringes used, handle minimally. Do not turn stopcock to reestablish IV infusion through proximal port between injections: reduce or discontinue IV flow through VIP port.
	Magnetic interference producing numerous spikes in CO curve	Try to determine cause of interference. Wipe CO computer with damp cloth.
	Long lag time between injection and upstroke of curve	Press "START" button *after* injection completed to delay computer sampling time.
Irregular upslope of CO curve	Uneven injection technique	Inject smoothly and quickly (10 ml in ≤ 4 sec).
	RA port partially occluded with clot	Always withdraw, then flush proximal port before CO determinations.
	Catheter partially kinked	Check for kinks, particularly at insertion site; straighten catheter, reposition patient.

Problem	Cause	Action
Irregular downslope of CO curve	Cardiac arrhythmias (PVCs, atrial fibrillation, etc.)	Note ECG during CO determinations. Try to inject during a stable period. Increase the number of CO determinations.
	Marked movement of catheter tip	Obtain X-ray film to determine position of tip. Advance catheter tip away from pulmonic valve.
	Marked variation in PA baseline temperature	Use iced temperature injectate to increase signal/noise ratio. Increase the number of CO determinations. Inject at various times during respiratory cycle.
	Curve prematurely terminated	Press START button *after* injection completed to delay computer sampling time.
	Right-to-left shunt	Use alternative CO measurement technique.

Cardiac Output

9 Circulatory Assist: Intraaortic Balloon Pumps (IABPs)

IABP

CIRCULATORY ASSIST: COUNTERPULSATION TECHNIQUE (INTRAAORTIC BALLOON PUMP) (IABP)

Definition

A method of assisting a patient's circulation.

Purpose

$\uparrow$ O_2 supply to myocardium during diastole
$\downarrow$ O_2 demand by myocardium during systole

Possible secondary effects:

Increased	Decreased
CO/CI	HR
Systemic perfusion	PADP
Urinary output	PAWP

Indications

Adjunct to mechanical ventricular-assist device
Cardiac transplantation
Cardiogenic shock (LVF) from:
    Acute MI
    Decreased CO states
    Post op surgery
Drug-induced CV failure
Drug-resistant arrhythmias
Pre-op maintenance:
    Papillary muscle rupture
    Ventricular aneurysms
    VSD from MI
Post-op assist:
    Cardiopulmonary bypass
Prophylactic during diagnostic studies
Septic shock
Thrombolytic therapy
Unstable angina pectoris (refractory)

Contraindications

Aortic valve incompetency
Chronic end stage heart disease (not on transplant list)
Dissecting thoracic aortic aneurysm
Severe peripheral vascular disease

An intraaortic balloon on a vascular catheter is inserted into the descending aorta via the femoral artery.

The balloon is positioned just inferior to the Ⓛ subclavian artery and superior to the renal arteries.

An intraaortic balloon pump (IABP) inflates the balloon with CO_2 or He gas during cardiac diastole.

A) INFLATION:
Diastolic augmentation
The inflated balloon creates a retrograde blood flow resulting in:
↑ BP dia in aortic arch
↑ coronary perfusion (↑ myocardial O_2 supply)
↑ $\overline{BP}$
↑ systemic perfusion
↑ O_2 supply

The pump then deflates the balloon during cardiac systole.

B) DEFLATION:
Afterload reduction (systemic unloading)
As blood from the arch flows into the void created by the deflated balloon:
↓ blood volume and pressure in arch
↓ afterload (↓ myocardial O_2 demand)
↑ SV
slight ↓ BP sys
↓ systolic ejection time (↑ diastolic time)
↑ coronary perfusion

A   **B**

IAB & IABP
EKG monitor
Aortic waveform monitor

Insertion technique

(beyond the scope of this book)

Operation of IABP

(Follow specific manufacturer's recommendations.)

General Guidelines

Monitor aortic pressure via central lumen of IAB catheter.
Insure aortic waveform has a distinct dicrotic notch.
Insure EKG has a tall (0.2 mV) positive R wave.

Timing

Timing is best set by the aortic pressure waveform, not by the EKG. (Need PP > 20 mmHg)
Proper timing is best achieved using a 1:2 frequency (every other beat).

Inflation timing

Immediately after aortic valve closure (dicrotic notch) to before opening of aortic valve (just prior to end diastolic pressure). (Usually just after T wave on EKG.)

Deflation timing

Just before aortic valve opens (end diastolic pressure) to when aortic valve closes (dicrotic notch). (Usually coincides with the QRS on EKG.)

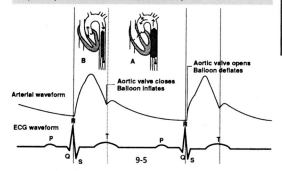

9-5

Interpretation of Arterial Waveform with IABP Assistance

Normal waveform

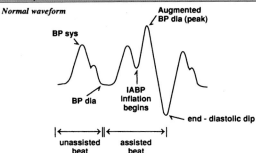

Optimal augmentation occurs when:
1. Inflation occurs at dicrotic notch
2. Inflation slope is parallel to arterial upstroke
3. Assisted BP dia (peak) > unassisted BP sys (see b in figure below)
4. Assisted BP dia (end) is 5-15 mHg lower than unassisted BP dia (end) (see c in figure below)

Optimal deflation occurs when:
Assisted BP sys < unassisted BP sys (see a in figure below)

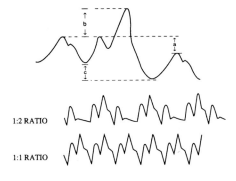

Abnormal waveforms

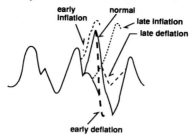

Clinical Notes Concerning Timing

Balloon pumping is most effective with HR of 80-120/minute.

In the presence of:

Tachycardia — (HR > 120) —	use helium gas. ↓ frequency to 1:3
Atrial fibrillation —	adjust augmentation sequence to shortest R-R interval. Deflation should occur on peak of R wave.
Ventricular fibrillation —	discontinue pump for a few seconds during delivery of defibrillation.
Cardiac arrest —	continue pump. Insure regular compression rate.

IABP

Parameter	q 15 min 1st hr	q30 min until stable	q hr until stable	q hr	q 2 hr	q 4 hr	q 8 hr
Hemodynamics							
BP sys, dia							
BP augmented diastolic		×			×		
RA, PA, PAWP							
CO, CI							
SVR, SVRI							
SW, SWI							
Vital Signs							
HR, RR, Temp			×			×	
Sounds							
Breath sounds					×		
Heart sounds							
Circulation							
Peripheral — pulses	×	×			×		
color							
temp							
etc.							
Cerebral — mental status				×			
Renal — UO				×			
Blood							
Platelets							×
ABG							
S$\bar{v}$O$_2$							

Header spanning row: **Monitoring times (or PRN)**

Precautions —
  Do not allow patient to sit up > 30° for x-ray, etc.
  Do not allow hip flexion of balloon extremity.

IABP

COMPLICATIONS OF THE INTRA-AORTIC BALLOON PUMP

Complication	Incidence	Prevention
Circulatory insufficiency of the catheterized limb distal to the insertion site	Most frequent	Use the largest femoral artery with the best pulse for balloon insertion. Administer heparin for anticoagulation. Frequently check the limb for signs of decreased circulation (temperature, color, pulses, movement, and sensation). When the balloon is removed, explore the femoral artery with a Fogarty catheter to remove clots.
Aortic or arterial damage (dissection, intimal laceration, or hematoma)	Occasional	Position the balloon catheter in the descending aorta just distal to the left subclavian artery. Select the correct balloon size, so that the inflated balloon does not occlude the aorta. Never advance the balloon-catheter if resistance is felt. Do not elevate head of bed > 30 degrees; limit patient movement (leg flexion can move the balloon tip up in the aorta, resulting in possible puncture of the arch).
Emboli from the balloon, catheter, sheath, or graft	Occasional	Administer heparin therapy. Do not leave the balloon in place if it is collapsed and motionless. Remove percutaneous sheath and catheter together.

IABP

9-9

Complication	Incidence	Prevention
Infection	Occasional	Allow wound to bleed vigorously 1 to 2 sec after removal of percutaneous balloon catheter. Use aseptic technique. Care for wound daily. Use prophylactic antibiotics. Change IV tubing every 24 to 48 hr.
Hemolysis	Minimal	Select the correct balloon size, so that the inflated balloon does not occlude aorta.
Platelet reduction	Frequent	Unknown; heparin may help.
Balloon leak or rupture with gas embolism	Rare	Use careful insertion technique to prevent damage to the balloon. Use carbon dioxide as the inflation gas since it is more soluble in blood. Choose the largest femoral artery for insertion.
Pseudoaneurysm or hematoma	Rare	Direct mechanical pressure at puncture site for 30 to 60 min after balloon removal.
Bleeding at puncture site	Occasional	Same as above.

Reprinted with permission from Daily, E.K. and Schroeder, J.S.: *Techniques in Bedside Hemodynamic Monitoring*, 4th Ed. Copyright 1989 by C.V. Mosby Co., St. Louis.

IABP TROUBLE SHOOTING GUIDE

Problem	Causes	Interventions
A. Balloon deflating prematurely	1. Premature ventricular contractions (PVCs)	1. Treat dysrhythmias
	2. Atrial fibrillation	2. a. Time to most common R-R intervals b. Deflation point to far right for automatic deflation at every R wave c. Restore to sinus rhythm, with appropriate therapy
	3. Atrial pacer spikes sensed as R waves	3. a. Choose lead with spike in opposite direction b. Bipolar pacing, with smaller spikes c. Swtich to arterial pressure trigger
B. Reduced diastolic augmentation	1. Tachycardia	1. a. Inflate earlier b. Disable inflation delay for earliest inflation time c. Decrease to 1:2 inflation frequency mode to allow time for inflation and deflation
	2. Improvement in the patient's own perfusion pressure	2. Physician may decide to begin weaning of balloon support
	3. Overdamping	3. a. Check for air bubble, cracks, or leaks in system. Tighten all connections b. Aspirate flush to make sure clot is not cause. Flush line, if patent
	4. Time to refill balloon	4. Refill balloon q 2 h. Note change in height of diastolic augmentation

Problem	Causes	Interventions
	5. Downward migration of IABP catheter	5. a. Immobilize cannulated leg b. Monitor for complaints of flank pain, decreased urine output, and other signs of renal artery occlusion c. Stat chest x-ray, if suspected d. Notify physician, who may need to readjust position of catheter
	6. Balloon not fully extended out of introducer sheath	6. a. Portable chest x-ray to verify catheter position b. Physician may need to advance catheter through sheath
C. Inaccurately high systolic and low diastolic monitor pressures	1. Underdamping	1. a. Recalibrate transducer b. A sealed air bubble device is available that reduces the overshoot of the pressure signal
D. Damped or loss of left arterial pressure waveform	1. Upward migration of catheter, occluding left subclavian or carotid artery	1. a. HOB flat b. Monitor left arm for circulatory changes c. Monitor patient for any neurologic changes d. Stat chest x-ray e. Notify physician
E. Diminished pulses of cannulated leg	1. Asymptomatic loss of distal pulses 2. Thrombus or embolus	1. Continue to monitor. Pulses usually return when the IABP is removed 2. a. Monitor quality of pulses, color, temperature, sensitivity, and ability to move toes b. Notify physician, who may need to outweigh the risk of losing a limb against the removal of the heart assist device

9-12

Problem	Causes	Interventions
		c. Prepare for removal of balloon, and possible placement in opposite extremity d. Prepare patient for surgical intervention, if this becomes necessary
F. Dormant catheter increases risk for clot formation	1. IABP console malfunction	1. a. Manually inflate and deflate balloon, with a 20-50 mL luer lock syringe every 5-15 min. Use at least 15 mL less fill gas or air (this is not counterpulsation, inflation could occur at systole) b. Replacement of IABP ASAP
G. Condensation	1. Water droplets collecting in safety chamber or extension tubing (does not affect IABP function, in small amounts)	1. a. Place pump on standby b. Disconnect at safety chamber or extension tubing c. Pump for 30 s with tubing or chamber faced downward to expel droplets d. Set pump back on standby e. Reconnect, refill, and resume pumping
H. Aortic dissection	1. Trauma during insertion or repositioning	1. a. Assess patient for lower abdominal or back pain, that may be radiating b. Monitor for increasing abdominal girth c. Note any new onset of inequality of pulses/blood pressure, between right and left side d. Stat chest x-ray e. Notify physician of suspicions f. Monitor patient for symptoms of shock

IABP

Problem	Causes	Interventions
I. Loss of augmentation	1. Kink or disconnection in extension tubing could result in loss of augmentation 2. Balloon leak	1. Unkink or secure loose connections Maintain some slack to prevent accidental disconnection 2. a. Monitor for frequent filling of balloon and wrinkles in safety chamber b. Stop pumping and place patient in deep Trendelenburg's position on left side, if gas embolus suspected
J. Appearance of blood in catheter	1. Balloon rupture	1. a. Stop pumping b. Clamp catheter, if blood backflow c. Notify physician and prepare for immediate removal of catheter
K. Loss of cardiac signal	1. Loose lead 2. Cardiac arrest	1. Obtain dependable ECG signal 2. a. If pacemaker present, turn on to proper setting. If pacemaker does not restore rhythm and defibrillation is necessary, turn pacer off and disconnect, if possible b. CPR c. May place IABP on arterial trigger, with CPR compressions serving as pressure signal d. Depending on your hospital policy, the internal trigger mode may be used to flutter balloon during cardiac arrest. The purpose of this is to prevent clot formation around the balloon

Reprinted with permission from Shoulders - Odom, "Managing the Challenge of IABP Therapy," *Critical Care Nurse: Vol. II #2*, p. 73. Copyright American Assoc. of Critical Care Nurses.

Criteria

Hemodynamic status	*Clinical status*
HR < 110	Good peripheral perfusion: Color, temp, pulses, mental status and UO.
CI > 2.0 L/min/m²	
	No significant arrhythmias.
BP > 70 mmHg (with minimal or no vasopressors)	No CHF.
PAWP < 18 mmHg	

Weaning

Techniques include:
- ↑ time off balloon
- ↓ balloon inflation volume (controversial)
- ↓ frequency of inflations (1:2, 1:4, 1:8, etc.)

(Technique used is highly variable and may take hours or days.)

IABP

Chapter Contents

(continued on next page)

Diseases

Diseases

ACUTE RESPIRATORY DISTRESS SYNDROME (ARDS) AND ACUTE LUNG INJURY (ALI)

Definition

An acute restrictive disease of diminishing FRC and severe hypoxia caused by injury to the alveolar – capillary membrane resulting in alveolar transudates, and ↓ surfactant, atelectasis, intrapulmonary shunting, ↑ $\dot{V}D$ and ↓ compliance.

Definition according to the American-European Consensus Conference on ARDS, 1994:

1) Acute onset of respiratory distress	3) Bilateral consolidation on CXR
2) Hypoxemia - *ARDS:* $PaO_2/FIO_2 \leq 200$ mmHg *ALI:* $PaO_2/FIO_2 \leq 300$ mmHg	4) Absence of clinical finding of cardiogenic pulmonary edema (PAOP < 18 mmHg or no LA hypertension)

Etiology

Respiratory (direct)	Non-Respiratory (indirect)
Aspiration	Blood transfusion reactions
Near-drowning	Burns (massive)
O_2 toxicity	DIC
Pneumonia (all types)	Drug abuse
Post-pneumonectomy	Fat embolism
Raised ICP (head injury)	Pancreatitis (acute)
Smoke inhalation	Prolonged cardiopulmonary bypass
Thoracic irradiation	Sepsis
Trauma (lung contusion/ injury)	Shock (severe and prolonged)
Vasculitis	

General Note:

The presence of pulmonary disease demands cautious interpretation of hemodynamic parameters.

Pulmonary disease that causes pulmonary hypertension (vasoconstriction from hypoxemia, acidemia, or obstruction) can profoundly affect cardiovascular function.

In increased PVR usually does not occur until > 50% of vascular bed is destroyed or obstructed.

The RV will normally produce an adequate CO up until PAMP > 35-45 mmHg (a chronic RV hypertrophy can produce PASP of 70-90 mmHg).

Pathophysiology:
<u>Overview</u>

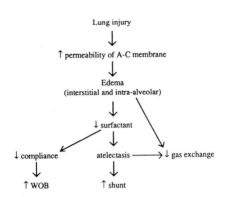

CLINICAL NOTE

ARDS vs. CHF

<u>ARDS</u>
Fluid in lungs (↑ cell permeability) = exudate (no initial ↑ PAP or ↑ PAWP)

<u>CHF</u>
Fluid in lung (↑ hydrostatic pressure) = transudate (immediate ↑ PAP and ↑ PAWP)

See Pulmonary Edema (Permeability)

Assessment ①

Clinical Manifestations		
Parameter/ Change		**Notes**
RR	↑	Cough, dyspnea
Breath sounds		Normal - early Rales & wheezes - late
ABG's		Hypoxemia Early - Resp. alk. Late - Resp. & metab. acid
HR	↑	
Pulse	N	
Heart sounds	N	
Neck veins	N	↑ if RHF
UO	↑/↓	
Skin	N	Late - pallor or cyanosis
Mental		Anxious Confusion Restless Late - obtunded

Hemodynamic Presentation		
Parameter/ Change		**Notes**
BP	↓/↑	
PP		Variable
CO	N	↓ late
CVP	N	↑ if RHF
PAP	↑	
PAWP	N	②
SVR	N	
PVR	↑	
S$\bar{v}$O$_2$	↓	hypoxemia

① Highly variable depending on stage of development.

② PAWP is normal in ARDS, but ↑ in pulmonary edema.

Diagnostic Studies

ABG's - refractory hypoxemia with progression from resp. alkalosis to resp. and metabolic acidosis.

PFT's - ↓ lung volumes (esp. FRC), ↓ lung compliance

X-ray - increasing diffuse bilateral infiltrates progressing to white out.

Management

Treat underlying cause

Prevent further A-C membrane damage

Maintain oxygenation and ventilation

Maintain hemodynamic stability and tissue perfusion

Diseases

CARDIAC FAILURE

Definition: The heart's inability to pump enough blood to meet tissue demands (also called **Congestive Heart Failure, CHF**)

Types: Left Heart Failure (LHF or LVF)
Right Heart Failure (RHF or RVF)
See also cardiogenic shock, cardiomyopathy, myocardial infarction, pulmonary edema, and valvular heart disease.

CLINICAL NOTE

The heart and vessels are a closed and continuous circuit, therefore, one side of the heart cannot pump more or less blood than the other without it eventually affecting the other side as well. Hence, failure of one side will ultimately produce failure of the other side.

Etiology: Many and varied:
1. Electrical abnormalities
2. Lung disorders (cor pulmonale)
3. Mechanical abnormalities
4. Myocardial abnormalities

Assessment

LEFT HEART FAILURE

Backward failure
↓ LV output
↓
pulmonary congestion①
(see pulmonary edema)

Forward failure
↓ LV output
↓
↓ systemic perfusion②
(see cardiogenic shock + MI)

Clinical manifestation	
↑ RR	SOB
Dyspnea	Hypoxemia
Cough	Crackles/wheeze
Orthopnea	$S_3 + S_4$
PND	Pulsus alternans
Pallor	

Clinical manifestation	
Cool, pale extremities	Fatigue
↓ Exercise tolerance	Anxiety
↓ Urinary output	S_3
Angina	

Hemodynamic presentation	
↑ PAD	↑ HR
↑ PAWP	↓ CO

Hemodynamic presentation	
↓ CO	Variable BP
↓ PP	↑ HR, ↑ SVR

Diseases

① LHF is most common cause of RHF (pulmonary congestion → ↓ RV output)
Note: As RH fails, there is a ↓ in pulmonary congestion resulting in a decrease in signs and symptoms and giving a false apparent improvement.

② ↓ Systemic perfusion → peripheral vasoconstriction → ↑ SVR → normal or ↑ BP to maintain cerebral and coronary perfusion
When ↓ CO > peripheral vasoconstriction, then →↓ BP → shock

RIGHT HEART FAILURE ①

Backward failure	**Forward failure**
↓ RV output	↓ RV output
↓	↓
venous congestion	↓ pulmonary perfusion
	↓
	↓ LV filling
	↓
	↓ LV output
	↓
	↓ systemic perfusion

Clinical manifestation

Jugular vein distension
Peripheral edema
Hepatomegaly
Fatique
Anorexia
Diaphoresis
S3
Kussmaul's sign
Pulsus paradoxicus

Hemodynamic presentation	**Clinical & hemodynamic presentations**
↑ CVP	Same as LHF (forward failure)

Diagnostic Studies:

ABG's	-	refractory hypoxemia
X-ray	-	pulmonary congestion
ECG	-	RV and/or LV hypertrophy arrhythmias
Angiography	-	abnormal wall motion and ejection fractions
Echocardiogram	-	RV or LV failure

Management:

Therapeutic intervention is based on the etiology and the hemodynamic alterations present. See cardiogenic shock, cardiomyopathy, myocardial infarction, pulmonary edema or valular heart disease

① RHF is called Cor pulmonale if due to lung disease.

Diseases

CARDIAC TAMPONADE

Definition: Acute and abnormal accumulation of fluid in pericardial sac resulting in heart compression.

Etiology:

Hemorrhage	Pericarditis	
Aneurysm	Infection	cardiac cath or surgery
Rupture	Radiation	anticoagulant therapy
Trauma or	SLE	MI
Surgery		neoplasm

Pathophysiology:

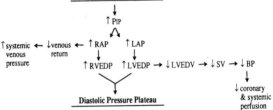

Abnormal Fluid Accumulation

↑ PIP

↑ systemic venous pressure ← ↓ venous return ← ↑ RAP   ↑ LAP

↑ RVEDP   ↑ LVEDP → ↓ LVEDV → ↓ SV → ↓ BP

↓ coronary & systemic perfusion

Diastolic Pressure Plateau

(RAP = RVEDP = PAD = PAWP = LAP = LVEDP)
This is a life-threatening situation
requiring immediate intervention

CLINICAL NOTE

Normal PIP = 3-5 mmHg (less than CVP)

Fluid accumulation needed for cardiac impairment:

    100-200cc if rapid (minutes to hours)

    1000-2000cc if slow (days)

Diseases

Assessment

CLINICAL NOTE
Parameters change proportional to the tamponade effect.

Clinical Manifestations

Parameter/ Change		Notes
RR	↑	dyspnea & orthopnea
Breath Sounds	N	
ABG's		Early → respiratory alkalosis Late → metabolic & resp. acidosis
HR	↑	↓ in late stage (ominous sign)
Pulse		Pulsus paradoxicus ① (classic finding) Weak (if severe tamponade)
Heart Sounds	↓	Muffled/inaudible ("silent heart")
Neck Veins	↑	↑ peripheral edema
UO	↑/↓	
Skin		Early — pale & warm Late — pale/ cyanosis and cool
Mental Status		Early — anxious Late — stupor

Hemodynamic Presentation

Parameter/ Change		Notes
BP sys BP dia PP	↓ ① N ↓	↓ BP (with ↑ CVP) during inspiration is diagnostic Damped waveform
CO	N/↓	↓ when compensatory mechanisms can no longer keep up
CVP PASP	↑ ② N	Proportional to PIP
PADP PAWP	↑ ② ↑ ②	Proportional to CVP ↓ PAD - PAWP gradient
SVR	↑	Compensation & proportional to ↓ SV
PVR	N/↑	↑ with hypoxemia/ acidosis
S⎺vO₂	N/↓	↓ with hypoxia and ↓ perfusion

Symptoms: Range from asymptomatic to total collapse
Include — dizziness
dyspnea
fullness in chest
retrosternal pain

---

① Pulsus paradoxus = ↓ BP sys > 10mmHg during inspiration (↑ on expiration).
Plus Kussmaul's sign: ↑ venous pressure (CVP) during inspiration (Venous waveform: a + v prominent, x + y descents are rapid)
Note: PPV may obscure these signs.

② These pressures eventually equalize to create the "Diastolic pressure plateau" (life threatening)

Diseases

Diagnostic Studies:

EKG   Variable depending on fluid accumulation level

CXR   Cardiac enlargement and globular shape
Clear lungs (this helps distinguish between tamponade and heart failure

Echocardiography   Diagnostic for pericardial effusion

Management:

Oxygen and ventilation therapy as needed

Maintain optimal cardiac output

Remove effusion — (definitive therapy).
Pericardiocentesis (only in life-threatening situations)
Surgery (Pericardiostomy or pericardiectomy)?

CARDIOMYOPATHY

Definition: Heart muscle disease of unknown cause characterized by decreased stroke volume, with or without ventricular dilation.

Etiology: Primary: Unknown
Secondary:
Associated with myocardial insults from —

Alcoholism	Malnutrition
Atherosclerosis	Pregnancy
Coronary artery occlusion	Sarcoidosis
Endocrine disorders	SLE
Genetic	etc.
Hypertension	
Immunologic or drug hypersensitivities	
Infection (many types)	

Pathophysiology:

Excessive ventricular dilation, stiffness and/or decreased filling → ↓ SV → CHF

Functional classification

1. Dilated (congestive): Dilation, but no hypertrophy of the ventricle, resulting in ↓ CO.

2. Hypertrophic (obstructive or IHSS): Abnormally stiff and hypertrophic LV resulting in ↓ filling (preload) and obstruction to outflow.

3. Restrictive (constrictive): Abnormally stiff walls from fibrosis resulting in ↓ filling (preload) due to ↓ cavity size.

Assessment

Clinical Manifestations ①		
Parameter/ Change		**Notes**
RR	↑	dyspnea if pulmonary congestion
Breath sounds	N	crackles if pulmonary edema
ABG's	N	respiratory alkalosis when hypoxemia occurs
HR	↑	often arrhythmic
Pulse	↓	Pulsus alternans
Heart sounds		S_4 S_3
Neck veins	↑	
UO	↓	
Skin		Pale, cool, maybe peripheral cyanosis
Mental status	N	

Symptoms: asymptomatic to total heart failure
    Include:
        DOE (1st sign)
        Orthopnea
        PND
        Fatigue
        Angina

Hemodynamic Presentation		
Parameter/ Change		**Notes**
BP sys BP dia PP	N ↑ ↓	damped waveform
CO	N/↓	
CVP	↑	due to ↑RVEDP waveform has prominent a wave
PASP	N/↑	damped waveform
PADP	N/↑	
PAWP	↑	due to ↑LVEDP
SVR	↑	compensation and proportional to ↓SV
PVR	N/↑	due to ↑LVEDP
S$\bar{\text{v}}$O$_2$	N/↓	↓ with ↓ in systemic perfusion

① These patients are highly prone to pulmonary and/or cerebral thrombi

Diagnostic Studies:

> **EKG —** LV hypertrophy
> Sinus tachycardia
> A-fibrillation (common and ominous sign)
> Various other arrhythmias
>
> **CXR —** Cardiac enlargement and pulmonary congestion
>
> **Echocardiography —** radionucleotide, catheterization and biopsy may be used to confirm diagnosis.

Management:

> Treat underlying cause if known
>
> Medical therapy is mostly supportive and will vary depending on disease type
>
> Maintain oxygenation and ventilation as needed
>
> Maintain optimal cardiac function
>
> IABP if myocardium is failing
>
> Surgery — correction or transplant?

CHRONIC OBSTRUCTIVE PULMONARY DISEASE (COPD)

Definition

A preventable and treatable disease with some significant extrapulmonary effects that may contribute to the severity in individual patients. Its pulmonary component is characterized by airflow limitation that is not fully reversible. The airflow limitation is usually progressive and associated with an abnormal inflammatory response of the lung to noxious particles or gases.

Asthma is not classified as COPD based on ATS Standards, 1995

Etiology

Chronic irritation (smoking, air pollution), infections (viral, bacterial), hereditary.

General Note:

The presence of pulmonary disease demands cautious interpretation of hemodynamic parameters.

Pulmonary disease that causes pulmonary hypertension (vasoconstriction from hypoxemia, acidemia, or obstruction) can profoundly affect cardiovascular function.

In increased PVR usually does not occur until > 50% of vascular bed is destroyed or obstructed.

The RV will normally produce an adequate CO up until PAMP > 35-45 mmHg (a chronic RV hypertrophy can produce PASP of 70-90 mmHg).

Diseases

Assessment ①

Clinical Manifestations			Hemodynamic Presentation		
Parameter/ Change		Notes	Parameter/ Change		Notes
RR	↑	labored	BP	N	varies with CO
Breath sounds	variable	depends on disease type and state	CO	N/↓	emphysema usually has a ↓ CO pattern, ↓ with RHF
ABG's	variable	emphysema (N) chronic bronchitis — compensated respiratory acidosis with hypoxemia	CVP	N ②	↑ with RHF (prominent a wave, quick x descent)
HR	↑		PASP	↑	proportional to PVR
Pulse	↑		PADP	↑	(hypoxemia, acidosis, obstruction, etc.)
Heart sounds		↑ pulmonic component of S_2			
Neck veins	N	↑ with RHF	PAWP	N	↑ only if LHD③ ↑ PAD - PAWP gradient
UO	N				
Skin	N	or cyanosis	SVR	N/↓	↓ is usually hypoxemia-induced vasodilation
Mental status	N	lethargy & confusion with hypoxemia	PVR	↑	hypoxemia-induced vasoconstriction
			$S\bar{v}O_2$	↓	proportional to hypoxemia and ↓ perfusion

Footnotes, ①, ②, ③ — see next page

Diseases

① Variable depending on disease type. The clinical picture of the COPD patient will change dramatically during acute exacerbations leading to acute respiratory failure (ARF).

Some causes of acute exacerbation		
Infection	↓ ventilation:	ascites
LVF		pain
Pulmonary		drugs
embolism		O_2 therapy — (↓ O_2 drive)

ARF may present the RH with a sudden pressure load which exceeds the work capacity of the RH.

② The heart of a COPD patient with an ↑ A-P diameter may not be in the mid-chest; hence the initial reference point may be inaccurate. Trends, therefore, are more important than absolute values.

③ Be cautious of "high" PAWP in COPD patients. They usually have enlarged zones 1 and 2, especially if pursed lip breathing. PAWP will be inaccurate if catheter tip is in zone 1 or 2. (See pg. 7-30)

Diagnostic Studies

Definitive: PFT's — airflow obstruction
Non-definitive: ABG's, ECG, CBC, electrolytes, X-rays

Management

Variable depending on disease type
Treat or remove underlying cause if possible
Reverse airway obstruction if possible
Maintain proper oxygenation and ventilation
Maintain proper bronchial hygiene
Maintain hemodynamic stability

Diseases

MYOCARDIAL INFARCTION, ACUTE

Definition: Acute myocardial ischemia resulting in necrosis of muscle tissue

Etiology: Coronary artery disease or ↓ coronary perfusion pressure

Pathophysiology:

↓ perfusion → ↓ O_2 supply → ↓ contractility → ↓ CO

Zones of Anatomic or Functional Loss

Necrosis	Injury	Ischemia
No O_2 or blood supply	Little or no O_2 and blood supply	Minimal O_2 and blood supply
Noncontractile	Noncontractile	Poor contractility
Electrically inert	Electrically unstable (arrhythmias)	Electrically unstable (arrhythmias)
ECG = deep or wide Q wave	ECG = elevated ST segment	ECG = inverted T-wave

Note: Myocardial cells begin to die (necrosis) if ischemic areas are not reperfused within 20 minutes.

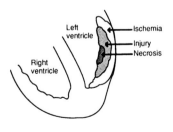

Assessment

Clinical Manifestations ①		
Parameter/ Change		**Notes**
RR	N	↑ with pain or pulmonary edema
Breath sounds	N	crackles with pulmonary edema ②
ABG's	N	Resp. alkalosis with anxiety, pain and/or pulmonary edema
		Metabolic acidosis with severe perfusion failure
HR	↑	anxiety, pain, pulmonary edema, etc.
	↕	arrhythmias
Pulse	N	↓ with heart failure
Heart sounds		S_4 S_3 (with heart failure)
Neck veins	N	Collapsed if supine and hypovolemic Distended if RHF
UO	N	↓ if cardiogenic shock
Skin		variable
Mental status		anxiety, dizzy nausea

Hemodynamic Presentation ③		
Parameter/ Change		**Notes**
BP	↑↓	↑ with SNS stimulation ↓ if ↓ CO or hypovolemic
PP	↓	possible pulsus alternans
CO	N ④	↓ if LHF
CVP	N	↓ if hypovolemic ↑ if RHF
PASP	N	↑ if LHF
PADP	N	↑ if LHF
PAWP	N ⑤	↓ if hypovolemic ↑ if LVF
SVR	↑↓	↑ with CNS stimulation ↑ if LHF
PVR	N	↑ with hypoxemia or pulmonary edema
$S\bar{v}O_2$	N	↓ if ↓ CO

Footnotes: See next two pages

Diseases

① Other findings may include: chest and radiating pain, nausea, vomiting and orthopnea.

② **The Killip Scale:** Hemodynamic Classification based on clinical exam.

Class	Description	Prevalence (%)	Mortality (%)
I	No pulmonary rales or S_3	33	6
II	Bibasilar rales which persist after cough, and/or an S_3	38	17
III	Rales over one half of the lung fields, with pulmonary edema on chest radiography	10	38
IV	Pulmonary edema with cardiogenic shock	19	81

Killip, T. and Kimball, J.: Am J. Cardiol 20:457, 1967.

③ **CLINICAL NOTE**

Hemodynamic presentation is dependent on and proportional to:
1. Location of damage
2. Extent of damage
3. Residual myocardial function

Prognosis is proportional to residual myocardial function
Cardiogenic shock or pump failure occurs when ≥ 40% of LV is infarcted.

Mortality is proportional to hemodynamic status at time of hospitalization.

High mortality exists when: PAWP >18 mmHg
Pulmonary congestion
Peripheral hypoperfusion

Hemodynamic classification based on Invasive Monitoring

Subset	Major Clinical Problem	PAWP	Management
I	Normal	< 18 mmHg	Conventional medical therapy
II	LV dysfunction	≥ 18 mmHg	Digitalis to ↑ contractility Diuretic to ↓ PAWP to < 18 mmHg Vasodilator to ↓ afterload
III	Peripheral hypoperfusion	< 18 mmHg	Volume loading for optimal preload
IV	LV dysfunction + peripheral hypoperfusion + pulmonary congestion	≥ 18 mmHg	Complex manipulations required

④ Use CI to determine magnitude of peripheral hypoperfusion

2.7-4.3	L/min	normal
2.2-2.7	L/min	subclinical depression of CO
1.8-2.2	L/min	onset of clinical hypoperfusion
< 1.8	L/min	cardiogenic shock

⑤ Use PAWP to determine magnitude of pulmonary congestion

4-12 mmHg	normal
12-18 mmHg	↑ PAWP usually without pulmonary congestion
18-20 mmHg	onset of pulmonary congestion
20-25 mmHg	moderate pulmonary congestion
25-30 mmHg	severe pulmonary congestion
> 30 mmHg	onset of pulmonary edema

(Pulmonary congestion can occur at normal PAWP if pulmonary capillaries are damaged [ie: "leaky," as in ARDS].)

Note: Use CI + PAWP to determine LV function (class) (see below)

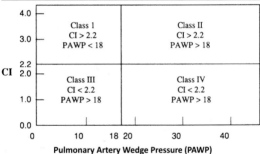

Pulmonary Artery Wedge Pressure (PAWP)

Clinical interpretation of FORRESTER classification					
Class	CI	PAWP	Pulmonary congestion	Peripheral hypoperfusion	Estimated mortality rate
I	normal	normal	no	no	±1%
II	normal	high	yes	no	±11%
III	low	normal	no	yes	±18%
IV	low	high	yes	yes	± 60%

Above modified from Forrester, J.S. et al: *Amer J. Cardiology* 39(2): 137-145, 1977.

Diseases

MI Classification based on V-function curves (LVSWI vs. PAWP)

Classification	Hemodynamic Presentation	Management
Normal	N SW N PAWP	No therapy
Group 1	↓ SW (slight) ↑ PAWP (slight)	No therapy
Group 2	↓ SW ↑ PAWP	Maintain PAWP to optimize SW and avoid pulmonary congestion
Group 3	<u>Cardiogenic shock</u> ↓ SW (↓ CO) ↑↑ PAWP (marked with pulmonary edema)	Maintain PAWP ↑ contractility (shifts curve up) ↓ afterload to ↑ CO
Group 4	<u>Cardiogenic and hypovolemic shock</u> ↓ SW ↓ PAWP	Careful and slow volume expansion
Group 5	<u>Hyperdynamic state</u> ↑ SW N PAWP	Reduce / eliminate cause: hypertension anxiety pain

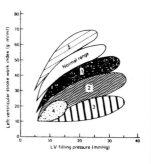

Adapted from Walinsky, P.: acute hemodynamic monitoring. *Heart and Lung* 6:840, 1977

Diseases

10-21

Diagnostic Studies:

Blood tests— ↑ WBC count, sedimentation rate, and blood glucose by second day.

Cardiac catheterization —
Helps define coronary artery spasm vs. fixed obstruction.

CXR — Cardiac enlargement and pulmonary congestion may precede clinical manifestations of heart failure.

ECG — Usually diagnostic.

> *Caution:*
> ECG changes may not occur even with significant injury. T-wave and ST changes are nonspecific and may not occur for up to one week.

Echocardiography —
Shows abnormal wall or papillary muscle movement. Ventriculograms — assess wall motion for abnormalities.

Radionuclide studies —
Technetium, thallium, pyrophosphate, ventriculography, etc.

Serum enzymes —
Abnormal concentrations following an MI.

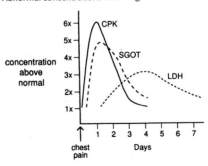

Management:

Goals		Methods
Limit infarct size:	Maintain O_2 supply > O_2 demand	↑ Myocardial O_2 supply — Eliminate blockage — pharmacotherapy angioplasty CABG ↓ Myocardial (X demand — (see below)
Maintain optimal cardiac function:	Maintain electrical stability	Treat arrhythmias (anti-arrhythmic agents) (Note: 90% exhibit arrhythmia in 1st 72 hrs.) ↓ Factors causing instability — acidosis anxiety fear hypoxia metabolic abnormalities pain
	Maintain adequate coronary perfusion	Ensure normal HR and rhythm Vasodilator therapy
	Maintain adequate peripheral perfusion	Ensure adequate CO + SVR IABP
	Decrease myocardial O_2 demand (↓ workload)	↓ HR and arrhythmias ↓ preload ↓ afterload ↓ contractility ↓ physical activity
Relieve pain		Analgesia and sedation
Prevent and treat complications:	↓ cell injury	Ca channel antagonists, hydrogen receptors, O_2 free radicals
	Pulmonary congestion	Maintain normal PAWP
	Dissolve coronary thrombosis	Thrombolytic therapy (streptokinase)
	Prevent thrombo-embolism (Pulmonary emboli or infarct)	Anticoagulant therapy (heparin, aspirin, TPA)

POST OP CARDIAC SURGERY

Definition: The cardiac surgery patient

Etiology: Cardiac surgery

Pathophysiology:

Effects of Surgery and Anesthesia

Effect	Causes
Respiratory depression	Anesthetic agents & drugs (morphine, diazepam)
Myocardial depression	Anesthetic agents
	Ischemia —
	Physiological stress: intubation
	Hypovolemia
	Prolonged induced V-fib.
	Aortic cross clamping
	Hypothermia

Whole body hypothermia

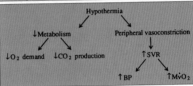

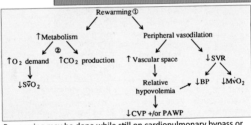

① Rewarming may be done while still on cardiopulmonary bypass or after return to SICU.

② **Caution:** A normal $PaCO_2$ of 40 mmHg and PaO_2 of 80 mmHg prior to rewarming may result in a rapid change to hypoxia and respiratory acidosis during rewarming.

Maintain slight hyperoxemia ($PaO_2 > 100$ mmHg) and a slight respiratory alkalosis ($\downarrow PaCO_2 + \uparrow pH$) in anticipation of the rapid increase in metabolism.

Shivering ($\uparrow O_2$ use and $\uparrow CO_2$ production) should also be controlled.

Diseases

Assessment

Clinical manifestations and hemodynamic presentations are highly variable dependent mostly on pathology being corrected.

Management

Maintain proper myocardial O_2 supply/demand balance

> **Note:** This O_2 balance is the major determinant of post-op morbidity and mortality.

Restore ventilatory independence.
    Acid-base balance
    Gas exchange
    WOB

Complications to watch for

Arrhythmias (hypoxemia, hypokalemia, CV drugs)
Cardiac tamponade
CNS complications (emboli, ↓ BP, delirium, ↓ sleep)
Embolization
Hemorrhage
LVF (anesthetics, ischemia, hypothermia)
↑ WOB (thoracotomy, pain, shivering, ↓ surfactant, pulmonary congestion, ↑ secretions)

PULMONARY EDEMA

Definition: Abnormal accumulation of fluid outside the vascular space of the lung

Etiology:

Two major types: (each will be addressed separately)

High pressure pulmonary edema (cardiogenic, hydrostatic)
Permeability pulmonary edema (noncardiogenic or neurogenic)

Pathophysiology (General)

Colloid osmotic pressure (COP) = force keeping fluid in vessels
COP normal = 28 mmHg

Pulmonary capillary hydrostatic pressure (PCHP) = force moving fluid out of vessels
PCHP normal = 6-15 mmHg

PCHP ≈ pulmonary venous pressure ≈ PAD ≈ PAWP ≈ LAP ≈ LVEDP

PCHP is the primary determinant of fluid shift from capillary into lung tissue. Estimate by PAWP.

COP – PAWP gradient = predisposition to edema COP < PAWP = edema

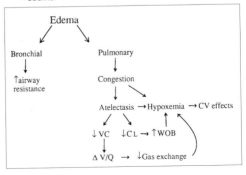

Three Phases of Progression

Phase	Pathology	Clinical Picture
Phase 1: Increased pulmonary fluid dynamics	↑ fluid movement from pulmonary capillaries to lung tissue. Lymph drainage increases to compensate.	Normal This phase may resolve, stabilize or go on to Phase 2.
Phase 2: Interstitial edema	Fluid movement from capillaries exceeds lymph drainage.	Mild ↑ RR X-ray — hazy lung fields poor definition of vascular markings Kerley B lines
Phase 3: Pulmonary edema	Fluid moves into alveoli	<u>Early</u> — ↑ RR fine crackles respiratory alkalosis X-ray — patchy, fluffy opacities <u>Late</u>— ↑ RR ↑ HR Labored breathing coarse crackles wheeze pulmonary edema froth respiratory acidosis

Diseases

High Pressure Pulmonary Edema (cardiogenic, hydrostatic)

Definition: Pulmonary edema due to a volume/pressure overload of the pulmonary circulation (Most common type of pulmonary edema)

Etiology:

Cause	Pathology	Disease examples
Intravascular volume overload	↑ intake ↓ output	excessive intake or infusion renal failure
Increased pulmonary venous pressure	obstructed pulmonary veins	mediastinal tumor venous occlusive disease
Increased LAP	LV inflow obstruction	mitral stenosis or regurgitation LA myxoma
Increased LVEDP (cardiogenic)	LV dysfunction (Most common cause of high pressure pulmonary edema)	acute MI aortic stenosis or regurgitation/arrhythmias cardiomyopathy/ constrictive pericarditis/hypertension /infection/physical exertion et cetera

Pathophysiology (specific)

↑ volume
↑ pressure
    venous
    LA   ⟶ ↑ PAWP → ↑ PCHP > COP → edema
    LVEDP

PAWP > 18-20 mmHg — gradual movement into lungs (onset of pulmonary congestion)

PAWP > 30-35 mmHg — rapid movement into lungs (acute pulmonary congestion)

Exceptions:

1. Chronic pulmonary hypertension where patients can tolerate higher pressures (eg. mitral stenosis)
2. Patients with ↓ plasma proteins develop edema at lower pressures
3. Increased capillary permeability (see Pg. 10-31)

Assessment (Phase 3)

Clinical Manifestations			Hemodynamic Presentation		
Parameter/ Change		**Notes**	**Parameter/ Change**		**Notes**
RR	↑	shallow, labored, nasal flare, retractions	BP	↑	↓ if in shock, waveform possibly damped
Breath sounds	rales	progresses from fine to gurgling wheezes	PP	N/↓	
			CO	N	LV dysfunction ↑ if ↑ intravascular volume overload or ↑ CO state
ABG's		Resp. alkalosis progresses to resp. and metabolic acidosis hypoxemia			
			CVP	N	↑ when RV fails against the ↑ PVR (usually when PAMP > 35 mmHg)
HR	↑				
Pulse	weak	bounding in ↑ CO states	PASP PADP	↑ ↑	waveform damped, giant v-wave in mitral regurgitation
Heart sounds		S₃ S₄ Summation gallop			
			PAWP	↑	
			SVR	↑	systemic induced vasoconstriction
Neck veins	N	distended if RHF			
UO	N/↓	↓ renal perfusion	PVR	↑	pulmonary vasoconstriction from hypoxemia
Skin		cool, clammy, peripheral cyanosis, warm & pink if ↑ CO state	Sv̄O₂	↓	↓ with hypoxemia or ↓ perfusion
Mental status		extreme anxiety, obtunded			

Diseases

Diagnostic Studies

    EKG —   variable, depending on cause

    X-Ray —   butterfly wing
              ↑ heart size if LVF
              (X-ray findings usually lag behind clinical
              manifestations during onset and resolution)

Management

    Treat underlying cause

    Maintain oxygenation and ventilation

    Patient position — Fowler's or sitting with feet down.

    Maintain optimal CO

    Treat anxiety —
        Morphine or sedation (anxietolytic) (watch for resp.
           depression)
        (Avoid if COPD)

Permeability Pulmonary Edema (non-cardiogenic or neurogenic)

Definition: Pulmonary edema due to an increased permeability of the pulmonary capillary membrane

Etiology:

Non-cardiogenic	*Neurogenic*
ARDS:	
Aspiration	Cerebral hemorrhage
Drug ingestion	Increased intracranial pressure
Infection	Stroke
Inhalation of toxins	Tumors
Metabolic disorders	Trauma to CNS
Pancreatitis	
Shock	
Trauma to chest or long bones (with fat emboli)	

Pathophysiology: (specific) (see also Pg. 10-4)

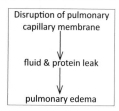

Disruption of pulmonary
capillary membrane

fluid & protein leak

pulmonary edema

Assessment — see next page

Management

Correct primary cause

Provide support (no therapy available to stop the disease progression; it must resolve itself)

Maintain proper oxygenation and ventilation

Diseases

Assessment (Four Clinical Stages)

Clinical Manifestation	Hemodynamic Presentation
Stage 1 — Injury No respiratory distress (unless trauma) ABG's — respiratory alkalosis from stress, slight hypoxemia, (PaO_2 70-80 mmHg) $S\bar{v}O_2$ normal X-ray — normal	Specific to cause Often within normal limits
Stage 2 — Latent period (12-48 hrs.) No respiratory distress ABG's — ↑ respiratory alkalosis, moderate hypoxemia (PaO_2 60-80 mmHg) $S\bar{v}O_2$ ↓ (proportional to ↓ SaO_2) X-ray — normal	Often still within normal limits
Stage 3 — Acute respiratory failure Acute respiratory distress ABG's — respiratory alkalosis may begin moving towards respiratory acidosis, severe hypoxemia (PaO_2 50-60 mmHg on room air) $S\bar{v}O_2$ continues to ↓ X-ray — diffuse infiltrates	May still be within normal limits unless CV disease or heart failure May see gradual rise in: ↑ PASP ↑ PADP ↑ PADP - PAWP gradient
Stage 4 — Severe respiratory failure Respiratory distress worsens (↑PIP 70-80 cm H_2O if on PPV) ABG's — respiratory and metabolic acidosis (if no PPV), severe hypoxemia ($PaO_2 \approx 40$ mmHg on FIO_2 1.0) $S\bar{v}O_2$ ↓↓ Mentally obtunded	CO: N(↓ if RVF and ↑ PVR) CVP: N (↑ if RVF) ↑↑ PASP ↑↑ PADP PAWP: N/↓(if no LV dysfunction) ↑ PVR

Diseases

PULMONARY EMBOLISM & INFARCTION

Embolism: Blockage of part of pulmonary vascular bed by blood-borne material (eg: clot, foreign body, air, fat, tumor) sometimes causing infarction of pulmonary tissue.

Infarction: Necrosis of pulmonary parenchyma due to an obstruction of the pulmonary circulation.
(Most common pulmonary complication in hospital patients.)

Etiology: Blood clot (90%) (majority come from legs).
Air
Tumor
Fat

Predisposing factors
1. Venous stasis (immobility)
2. Vein disorder (varicose or atherosclerosis)
3. Vein damage (trauma)
4. Hypercoagulability

Pathophysiology

Embolism results in circulatory blockage, causing a cessation of blood flow distally.

Effects of this may inclue:

1. ↑ Deadspace ventilation (ventilation without perfusion).
2. Local vasoconstriction → ↓ local surfactant → atelectasis.
3. Pulmonary infarction.
4. Hemodynamic abnormalities
   a. ↑ PVR (usually only if > 50% of vascular bed is occluded)
   ↓
   ↑ PAP (PAWP remains normal)
   ↓
   ↑ RV afterload
   ↓
   ↑ RV work
   ↓
   Possible RV failure

Assessment

Note: Many findings may already be abnormal due to pre-existing cardiopulmonary disease.

Clinical Manifestations①		
Parameter/ Change		**Notes**
RR	↑	dyspnea, cough
Breath sounds	crackles	
ABG's		Resp. alkalosis with hypoxemia
HR	↑	pain, apprehension, hypoxemia
Pulse	variable	
Heart sounds	N	S_3/S_4 gallop?
Neck veins	N	distended if RHF
UO	N	
Skin	N	cyanosis?
Mental status	N	apprehension, pain, anxiety

Hemodynamic Presentation①		
Parameter/ Change		**Notes**
BP	N	↓ if massive
PP	N	↓ if massive
CO	N	slight ↑ with hypoxemia, ↓ if massive
CVP	N	↑ if RHF (↑ a wave)
PASP	↑	if ↑ PVR,
PADP	↑	often is a diagnostic indicator
PAWP	N	↑ PAD - PAWP gradient ↓ PAWP if RHF
SVR	N	↑ if massive, due to ↓ CO
PVR	↑	if significant occlusion
SvO₂	N	↓ with hypoxia or ↓ perfusion

① Findings are highly variable and inconsistent. They are all relatively proportional to the degree of obstruction. Above represent the most common findings.

Other findings may include nausea, syncope, chest pain, and hemoptysis, diaphoresis

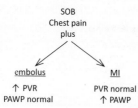

Pulmonary embolus vs. acute MI

SOB
Chest pain
plus

embolus   MI

↑ PVR   PVR normal
PAWP normal   ↑ PAWP

Diagnostic Studies

> **Note:** No definitive diagnostic test is yet available. The
> following can be very nonspecific due to the common
> presence of other abnormalities: ABG's, X-ray, ECG, CBC

Pulmonary angiography* —
  Most definitive (must be done within first 72 hours).

Lung ventilation/perfusion scan —
  ↓ Local areas of perfusion without associated ↓ ventilation.
  False positives are common due to other abnormalities.

Management

  Maintain proper oxygenation and ventilation
  Treat anxiety and pain
  Maintain hemodynamic stability
  Dissolve existing clot (thrombolytic therapy)
  Prevent future embolization (anticoagulant therapy)
  Embolectomy? (last resort)

SHOCK

Definition: Inadequate tissue perfusion resulting in a hypoxic insult and causing widespread abnormal cell metabolism and membrane dysfunction.

Etiology and Classification of Shock:

Hypovolemic
  Compensated
  Decompensated

Anaphylactic

Cardiogenic

Neurogenic

Septic (Vasogenic)
  Hyperdynamic (warm)
  Hypodynamic (cold)

HYPOVOLEMIC SHOCK

Definition: A decrease in the effective circulating blood volume (This is the most common form of shock)

Etiology: Hemorrhage (loss of whole blood)

Non-hemorrhage (loss from interstitial space)

Dehydration (vomiting, diarrhea, diuresis, diabetes, heat exhaustion, etc.)

Third space fluid shift (burns, trauma, sepsis, ascites, etc.)

Categories: Compensated — initial stage when BP is maintained by compensatory vasoconstriction

Decompensated — later stage when BP ↓ because ↓ volume is greater than the ability to compensate

Compensation is often effective up to ≈ 25% volume loss (ie: 1000ml in a 70kg man).

PATHOPHYSIOLOGY

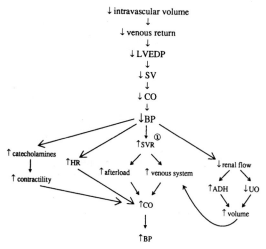

① Vasoconstriction occurs mainly in skin, renal and splanchnic vessels. Little or no constriction occurs in cardiac or cerebral vessels, hence blood flow is preferentially directed to the heart and brain.

Note, however, that prolonged vasoconstriction and decreased perfusion to the periphery usually results in biochemical changes leading to a furthering of the shock state.

Assessment (compensated)

Clinical Manifestations			Hemodynamic Presentation		
Parameter/ Change		**Notes**	**Parameter/ Change**		**Notes**
RR	↑		BP ①	N	↑ BPdia is one of 1st parameters to change
Breath sounds	N				
ABG's		resp. alkalosis and metabolic acidosis	PP	N/↓	
			CO	variable	⎫ all depend on
			CVP	variable	⎪ balance
			PASP	variable	⎬ between
HR	↑	> 100	PADP	variable	⎪ volume and
Pulse	N/↓	maybe pulsus paradoxicus	PAWP	variable	⎭ compensation
			SVR	↑	
Heart sounds	N		PVR	↑	
Neck veins		collapsed	S$\bar{v}$O$_2$	↓	hypoxemia and ↓ perfusion
UO	↓				
Skin		extremities: cool, pale and clammy trunk: warm and dry			
Capillary refill	↓				
Mental status		anxious obtunded			

① **Caution** — absolute values may be misleading.

BP is not a good indicator of overall status.

A ↓ BP sys has historically been a hallmark of shock, but ↓ CO, BPdia and ↓ PP usually occur long before a ↓ BP sys.

An ↑ BP sys, on the other hand, is not indicative of shock, yet large tissue beds may be underperfused due to vasoconstriction.

Diseases

Decompensated

(Loss > compensation)

Occurs generally when > 30% volume loss (1500 ml in 70kg man).

Assessment (decompensated)

Clinical Manifestations		
Parameter/ Change		**Notes**
RR	↑↑	may be blunted
Breath sounds	N	
ABG's		metabolic acidosis with or without resp. compensation
HR Pulse	↑	> 120 weak & thready
Heart sounds	N	
Neck veins		collapsed
UO Skin	↓↓	cool, clammy, ashen gray (all over)
Capillary refill	↓	
Mental status		extreme anxiety leading to obtunded and coma

Hemodynamic Presentation		
Parameter/ Change		**Notes**
BP	↓	↓ BP sys and ↓ BPdia
PP	↓	
CO	↓	
CVP	↓	
PASP	↓	
PADP	↓	
PAWP	↓	↑ PAD-PAWP gradient
SVR	↑	
PVR	N/↑	hypoxia and acidosis note — a large ↑ = poor prognosis
SvO$_2$	↓	

Management (Treatment of shock may be detrimental if the diagnosis is not precise.)
1. Correct primary problem — Stop blood or fluid loss.
2. Restore adequate tissue perfusion — Restore volume

Note: Clinical research continues on best choices and combinations of replacement solutions (ie: colloid vs. crystalloid or salt/sugar/water solutions only)

Trendelenburg position
Vasopressors
Oxygenation
MAST trousers?

ANAPHYLACTIC SHOCK

Definition: Systemic allergic reaction causing circulatory failure
and biochemical abnormalities.

Etiology: Anesthetics (local)
Antibiotics (various)
Anti-inflammatory agents (non-steroidal)
Blood and blood products
Diagnostic agents
Drugs (various)
Foods (various)
Hormones (various)
Narcotic analgesics
Pollens
Venoms

Pathophysiology — see Pg. 10-45

(Process started by allergic reaction rather than
toxins.)

Bronchoconstriction is a major consequence of this
reaction.

Assessment

Clinical Manifestations		
Parameter/ Change		**Notes**
RR	↑↑	rapid due to bronchocon- striction, mucosal edema & possible pulmonary edema
Breath sounds		wheezes, crackles if pulmonary edema
ABG's		resp. alkalosis with severe hypoxemia then resp. & metabolic acidosis
HR	↑	
Pulse	↓	weak & irregular
Heart sounds	N	
Neck veins	N	
UO	↓	
Skin	variable	
Mental status		anxiety, obtunded

Hemodynamic Presentation		
Parameter/ Change		**Notes**
BP	↓↓	↓ BP sys, ↓ BP dia
PP	↓	
CO	↓↓	initial ↑ then rapid ↓↓
CVP	↓	all
PASP	↓	due
PADP	↓	to
PAWP	↓	hypovolemia
SVR	↓	
PVR	N/↑	
S$\bar{v}$O$_2$	↓	hypoxemia and ↓ perfusion

Management

1. Remove antigen.
2. Maintain airway, O$_2$ and ventilation.
3. Treat bronchospasm.
4. Treat anaphylaxis. ⎫
5. Treat hypovolemia. ⎬ epinephrine, volume, vasopressors

10-41

CARDIOGENIC SHOCK

Definition: Systemic hypoperfusion due to profound heart failure
($\downarrow$ contractility) and/or its ability to meet metabolic
needs. Also called **Pump Failure**

> **Note:**
> *Clinical Definition:*
> 1. BP sys < 90 mmHg (or 25% lower than normal)
> 2. UO < 20 ml/hr.
> 3. Poor tissue perfusion —
>   cool, clammy, mottled skin
>   mental confusion, obtunded

Etiology: Final end stage of heart disease caused by:
  acute MI (> 40% infarction of LV) *most
      common cause
  acute myocarditis
  arrhythmias
  cardiac tamponade
  cardiomyopathy (end-stage)
  constrictive pericarditis
  mechanical dysfunction (ruptured papillary
      muscle or septum)
  post op failure
  pulmonary embolism (massive ruptured aortic
      aneurysm)
  severe depressed heart function
      (hypoxemia, acidemia, septicemia, etc.)
  severe valve dysfunction
  tension pneumothorax

Note: Mortality is very high

Pathophysiology: See Pg. 10-37 (beginning with $\downarrow$ CO)

Diseases

Assessment ①

Clinical Manifestations			Hemodynamic Presentation		
Parameter/Change		Notes	Parameter/Change		Notes
RR	↑↑	rapid and shallow	BP	↓↓	↓ BP sys, ↓ BP dia
Breath sounds	N/↓	crackles if pulmonary congestion	PP	↓	
			CO	↓	
ABG's		initial resp. alkalosis with hypoxemia, then resp. and metabolic acidosis	CVP	N	↑ if RH infarct or RHF
			PASP PADP PAWP	}	↑ if LH infarct ↓ if RH infarct
HR	↑	variable if arrhythmias, ↓ if LV ischemia	SVR	N/↑	
			PVR	N/↑	↑ due to hypoxemia and acidosis
Pulse	↓	weak & thready	S̄vO₂	↓	hypoxemia and ↓ perfusion
Heart sounds	N	variable if arrhythmia			
Neck veins	N	↑ if RHF			
UO Skin	↓	< 20ml/hr. cool, clammy, mottled			
Capillary refill	↓				
Mental status		confusion, obtunded			

① See myocardial infarction for assessment findings in the early stage of this disease.

Management

1. Treat cause
2. Maintain O₂ and ventilation
3. Optimize CO and tissue perfusion
4. IABP, CABG or transplant

Diseases

NEUROGENIC SHOCK

Definition: Dysfunction of sympathetic nervous system resulting in massive peripheral vasodilation and systemic hypoperfusion.

Etiology:
Trauma (brain or spinal cord)
Drugs (various)
Insulin shock
Spinal anesthesia
Pain

Pathophysiology: See Pg. 10-37

Assessment

Clinical Manifestations			Hemodynamic Presentation		
Parameter/ Change		**Notes**	**Parameter/ Change**		**Notes**
RR	variable	depends on cause and site	BP	↓	↓ BP sys & ↓ BP dia
			PP	↓	
Breath sounds	N		CO	N/↓	
ABG's	variable		CVP	↓	} due
HR	↓	* only shock with ↓ HR	PASP	↓	to
			PADP	↓	relative
Pulse	N/↓		PAWP	↓	hypovolemia
Heart sounds	N		SVR	↓	
Neck veins	N		PVR	N/↑	
			S$\bar{v}$O$_2$	↓	↓ perfusion
UO	↓				
Skin		warm & flushed			
Mental status	↓	lethargy to stupor			

Management

1. Treat the cause (if possible)
2. Maintain O$_2$ and ventilation
3. Treat relative hypovolemia due to vasodilation (vasopressors)

SEPTIC SHOCK (VASOGENIC)

Definition: Shock associated with any infectious disease which causes relative hypovolemia.

Etiology: Many infectious agents

> **Note:** Gram negative bacillus is the most common hospital-acquired infection.
>
> Gram positive organisms (ie: staphylococcus aureus or streptococcal species) are the most common IV line sepsis.

Predisposing factors
    Invasive procedures (including intubation)
    Organ damage
    Immunocompromised

Pathophysiology

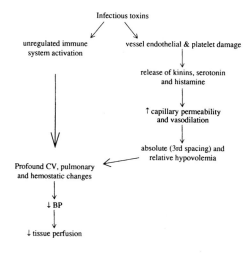

Infectious toxins

unregulated immune system activation

vessel endothelial & platelet damage

release of kinins, serotonin and histamine

↑ capillary permeability and vasodilation

absolute (3rd spacing) and relative hypovolemia

Profound CV, pulmonary and hemostatic changes

↓ BP

↓ tissue perfusion

Phases

1. Hyperdynamic — warm shock
2. Hypodynamic — cold shock

Hyperdynamic Phase (Warm Shock)

Early phase when heart ($\uparrow$CO) compensates for the $\downarrow$ BP ($\downarrow$ SVR)

Assessment

Clinical Manifestations			Hemodynamic Presentation		
Parameter/ Change		**Notes**	**Parameter/ Change**		**Notes**
RR	$\uparrow$		BP	N/$\downarrow$	
Breath sounds	N		PP	$\uparrow$	
ABG's		resp. alkalosis	CO	N/$\uparrow$	$\uparrow$ with $\downarrow$ afterload
HR	$\uparrow$		CVP	$\downarrow$	
Pulse	$\uparrow$	bounding	PASP	variable	changes
Heart sounds	N		PADP	variable	with
			PAWP	variable	Δ PVR
Neck veins	N		SVR	$\downarrow$	
UO	$\downarrow$		PVR	N/$\uparrow$	reason for $\uparrow$ is unknown. sign of poor prognosis.
Skin		warm, flushed, pink, dry	$S\overline{v}O2$	$\uparrow$	due to vasodilation
Capillary refill	N				
Mental status	variable				

Diseases

Hypodynamic Phase (Cold Shock)

Later phase when heart ($\uparrow$ CO) can no longer compensate for
$\downarrow$ BP ($\downarrow$ SVR).

Assessment

Clinical Manifestations			Hemodynamic Presentation		
Parameter/ Change		Notes	Parameter/ Change		Notes
RR	$\uparrow$	hypoventilation & possible altered breathing patterns	BP	$\downarrow$	
			PP	$\uparrow$	?
			CO	$\downarrow$	progressive $\downarrow$
Breath sounds	N		CVP	$\downarrow$	
ABG's		metabolic and resp. acidosis with hypoxemia	PASP PADP PAWP	$\uparrow$/$\downarrow$	$\downarrow$ if PVR normal $\uparrow$ if PVR increases
HR	$\uparrow$		SVR	variable	
Pulse	$\downarrow$	weak & thready	PVR	N/$\uparrow$	
Heart sounds	N		S$\bar{v}$O$_2$	variable	$\downarrow$ with $\downarrow$ perfusion, $\uparrow$ with abnormal O$_2$ utilization
Neck veins	N				
UO	$\downarrow$	anuria			
Skin		cold, clammy, pale, mottled, or cyanosis			
Capillary refill	$\downarrow$				
Mental status	$\downarrow$	progressing to stupor and coma			

Management

1. Restore adequate tissue perfusion — volume therapy
   oxygenation
   vasopressors

2. Eliminate cause of sepsis

3. Antibiotic therapy

Diseases

Relative position on ventricular function curve of different shock types

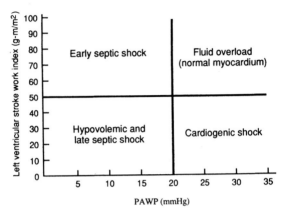

Reprinted with permission from Bustin, D., *Hemodynamic Monitoring for Critical Care*. Copyright 1986 by Appleton-Century-Crofts, Norwalk.

VALVULAR HEART DISEASE

Types: Stenosis or regurgitation

Valves: RH: Pulmonic   LH: Aortic
                    Tricuspid   Mitral

> **Note:** RH: Valve disease is rare, but increasing
>   with non-sterile IV drug users.
>   LH. Aortic disease > mitral disease.
>   Stenosis more common than regurgitation.

Valve diseases covered in this text —
        aortic stenosis
        aortic regurgitation
        mitral stenosis
        mitral regurgitation

Aortic Stenosis

Definition: Obstruction of flow from LV to aorta.

Etiology: Congenital abnormality
                    Degenerative (wear and tear)
                    Rheumatic fever

Pathophysiology

   Systole: $\uparrow$ LVSP (up to 300 mmHg) $\rightarrow$ $\uparrow$ M$\dot{v}O_2$
                    $\downarrow$ CO $\rightarrow$ LHF

Note:

> **Note:** Aortic valve gradient (AVG) =
>   LVSP − AoSP
>   (AVG > 50 mmHg = critical)

   Diastole: $\uparrow$ LVSP $\rightarrow$ $\uparrow$ ventricle mass $\rightarrow$ $\downarrow$
   myocardial compliance $\rightarrow$ LV dilates $\rightarrow$ $\uparrow$ LVEDP $\rightarrow$
   $\uparrow$ LAP $\rightarrow$ LHF $\rightarrow$ $\uparrow$ PAWP $\rightarrow$ Pulmonary edema $\rightarrow$
   $\uparrow$ RVP $\rightarrow$ $\uparrow$ RAP $\rightarrow$ RHF

> **Note:** Pulmonary edema is an ominous
>   sign and associated with rapid
>   clinical deterioration.

Diseases

10-49

Assessment

Clinical Manifestations ①		
Parameter/ Change		**Notes**
RR	↑	↑ with pulmonary edema
Lung sounds		crackles and wheeze with pulmonary edema
ABG's	N	until pulmonary edema
HR	↑	↑ as CO ↓
Pulse	↓	↓ as CO ↓
Heart sounds		systolic, harsh crescendo — decrescendo murmur
Neck veins	N	↑ if RHF
UO	N	
Skin	N	
Capillary refill	N	
Mental status	N	

Hemodynamic Presentation		
Parameter/ Change		**Notes**
BP	↓	↓ BP sys
PP	↓	damped waveform
CO	↓	
CVP	N/↑	↑ if RHF due to LHF
PASP	↑	
PADP	↑	
PAWP	↑	
SVR	↑	
PVR	↑	
SvO_2	↓	

① Clinical and hemodynamic parameters remain normal until LHF occurs.

Mild to moderate stenosis is asymptomatic.

When stenosis is severe (< 1/3 normal diameter), then patient exhibits fatigue, dyspnea, syncope and angina pectoris.

Diagnostic Studies — See Pg. 10-57

Management

Mild to moderate stenosis and asymptomatic: no specific therapy needed. (Prophylactic antibiotics?)

Severe (or AVG > 50) = surgery.

Diseases

Aortic Regurgitation

Definition: Incomplete closure of aortic valve resulting in retrograde blood flow from aorta into LV during diastole. (Also known as **aortic insufficiency**.)

Etiology: Dissecting aneurysm
Infection
Systemic inflammatory disease
Trauma

Pathophysiology:

Chronic, compensated

Gradual ↑ retrograde flow → ↑ LVEDV → ↑ LV size
↓
↑ LVSP
↓
↑ SV

↙   ↘

BP sys   ↑M$\dot{\text{V}}$O$_2$
+   ↓
↓ BP dia → ↓ CPP → Potential
                            ischemia

Chronic, decompensated

↑ retrograde flow and/or ischemia → ↓ contractility

↙   ↘

↑ LAP ← ↑ LVEDP ← ↑ LV compliance   ↓SV
↓   ↓
↑ PAWP → pulmonary edema   ↓ CO
+   ↓
↑ PAP → ↑ RH pressures → RHF   LHF
                                            ↓
                                          Shock

Acute (eg. trauma)

acute retrograde flow → ↓ SV → ↓ CO → LHF → shock
↓
↑ LVEDV → ↑ LVEDP → ↑ LAP → ↑ PAWP → acute pulmonary
                                                  edema

Diseases

Assessment

Clinical Manifestations				Hemodynamic Presentation		
	Change/Notes				**Change/Notes**	
Parameter	Chronic, Compensated	Acute or Decompensated		**Parameter**	Chronic, Compensated	Acute or Decompensated
RR	N	↑ with dyspnea and PND		BP sys	↑	↓↓
Lung sounds	N	crackles and wheeze with pulm edema		BP dia	↓	↓
ABG's	N	resp. alkalosis then resp. and metabolic acidosis		PP	↑	↓
				CO	N	↓
HR	N	↑		CVP	N	↑ with RHF
Pulse	bounding	↓ bounding		PASP	N	↑
Heart	blowing, high-pitched, decrescendo diastolic murmur			PADP	N	↑
				PAWP	N/↑	↑
Neck veins	N	↑ if RHF		SVR	N/↓	N/↑
UO	N	↓		PVR	N	↑ (with onset of pulm edema)
Skin	flushed diaphoretic	pale cyanotic				
Capillary refill	N	↓		$S\bar{v}O_2$	N	↓
Mental status	N	stuporous				

Diagnostic Studies — see Pg. 10-57

Management

Compensated:	No treatment needed (Prophylactic antibiotics?)
Decompensated:	Treat heart failure Surgery is definitive treatment
Acute:	Emergency surgery

Mitral Stenosis

Definition: Obstruction of flow from LA to LV.

Etiology: Carcinoid disease
Congenital abnormality
Infective endocarditis
Rheumatic fever (most common)

Pathophysiology

1. ↑ LAP (chronic or acute: from exercise, stress or ↑ HR)

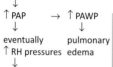

Note:	Chronic ↑ LAP results in an elevated pulmonary edema threshold due to: 1. hypertrophy of pulmonary arterioles (↑ PVR) 2. ↑ lymph flow 3. ↓ A-C memb permeability
Note:	Atrial fib is common as LA dilates.

2. ↓ LV fill
   ↓
   ↓ LV volume → ↓ LVSV → ↓ CO → ↓ exercise tolerance
   ↑ fatigue & weakness

Note:	↓ CO is fixed. It cannot increase in response to ↑ metabolic demands from exercise, fever or stress.

Assessment

Clinical Manifestations ①			Hemodynamic Presentation		
Parameter/ Change		**Notes**	**Parameter/ Change**		**Notes**
RR	N	↑ with pulmonary congestion. dyspnea is often 1st sign of disease. PND, orthopnea	BP	N	↓ if signif ↓ CO
			PP	↓	
			CO	N/↓	↓ proportional to obstruction
Lung sounds	N	crackles and wheeze if pulmonary edema	CVP	N/↑	↑ as RV fails
			PASP	N/↑	↑ as obstruction becomes more severe (PAWP reflects LAP but not LVEDP) PAWP > LVEDP ↑ PAD-PAWP gradient
ABG's	N	unless pulmonary edema or ↓ BP	PADP	N/↑	
			PAWP	N/↑	
HR	N/↑	A-fib is common			
Heart sounds		accentuated S_1 diastolic rumble	SVR	N/↑	↑ as CO ↓
Neck veins	N	↑ if RHF	PVR	N/↑↑	↑ with severity
Skin		pale and warm maybe cyanosis	SvO$_2$	N/↓	↓ if ↓ perfusion
Mental status	N				

① Onset of changes are gradual, first seen during exertion or stress.

Diagnostic Studies — see Pg. 10-57

Management

Asymptomatic — no treatment necessary (prophylactic antibiotics?)

Symptomatic — maintain optimal CO
treat arrhythmias (esp. to slow down rapid rates)
treat anxiety, stress
minimize activity
surgery

Diseases

Mitral Regurgitation

Definition: Incomplete closure of mitral valve, resulting in retrograde blood flow from LV into LA during systole (also known as **mitral insufficiency**).

Etiology: Bacterial endocarditis (sepsis)
Coronary artery disease
Ischemia of papillary muscle
LV dilatation (enlarges the valve ring annulus)
Marfan's syndrome
Mitral valve prolapse
Rheumatic fever
Trauma

Pathophysiology

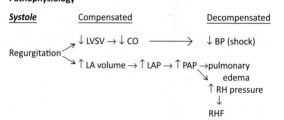

Systole	Compensated	Decompensated

Regurgitation → ↓ LVSV → ↓ CO ⟶ ↓ BP (shock)

Regurgitation → ↑ LA volume → ↑ LAP → ↑ PAP → pulmonary edema
↘ ↑ RH pressure
↓
RHF

Assessment

Clinical Manifestations		
	CHANGE/NOTES	
Para-meter	Chronic, Compensated	Acute Uncompensated
RR	↑, ortho-pnea	↑↑, dyspnea
Lung sounds	N	crackles & wheeze with pulm. edema
ABG's	N	resp. alkalosis then resp. & metabolic acidosis
HR	N/↑	↑, arrhythmias are common
Pulse	↓	↓↓ pulsus alternans with LV dysfunction
Heart Sounds	Blowing, high pitched holosystolic murmur, atrial and/or ventricular gallop	
Neck veins	N	↑ if RHF
UO	N	↓
Skin	pale & warm, cool extremities	cool & clammy, ashen with peripheral cyanosis
Capillary refill	N	↓
Mental status	alert, fatigued	obtunded, restless

Hemodynamic Presentation		
	CHANGE/NOTES	
Para-meter	Chronic, Compensated	Acute or Decompensated
BP	N	N/↑
PP	N	↓
CO	N	↓
CVP	N	↑ with RHF
PASP	↑	↑
PADP	↑	↑
PAWP	↑	↑ ①
	(↑ is proportional to ↑ LAP)	
SVR	N	↑ (prop. to ↓ CO)
PVR	N/↓	↑ (with onset of pulm. edema)
S͞vO₂	N	↓ ②

① ↑ PAWP (mean) is not representative of true LVEDP

PAWP (diastolic) may be proportional to LVEDP, but wide inaccuracies may occur

PAWP exhibits giant v waves

② Severe mitral regurgitation may cause a falsely elevated S͞vO₂

Diagnostic Studies - see Pg 10-57

Management

Chronic, compensated — no treatment needed.
Acute, uncompensated — treat heart failure and arrhythmias. Surgery if medical management fails.

Diseases

Findings in Valvular Heart Disorders

Disorder	Chest radiograph	ECG	Echocardiogram	Cardiac catheterization
Mitral stenosis	Left atrial enlargement Mitral valve calcification Right ventricular enlargement Prominence of pulmonary artery	Left atrial hypertrophy Right ventricular hypertrophy Atrial fibrillation	Thickened mitral valve Left atrial enlargement	Increased pressure gradient across valve Increased left atrial pressure Increased PCWP Increased right heart pressures Decreased CO
Mitral insufficiency	Left atrial enlargement Left ventricular enlargement	Left atrial hypertrophy Left ventricular hypertrophy Atrial fibrillation Sinus tachycardia	Abnormal mitral valve movement Left atrial enlargement	Mitral regurgitation Increased atrial pressure Increased LVEDP Increased PCWP Decreased cardiac output
Aortic stenosis	Left ventricular enlargement Aortic valve calcification May have enlargement of left atrium, pulmonary artery, right ventricle, right atrium	Left ventricular hypertrophy	Thickened aortic valve Thickened ventricular wall Abnormal movement of aortic leaflets	Increased pressure gradient across valve Increased LVEDP

Diseases

Disorder	Chest radiograph	ECG	Echocardiogram	Cardiac catheterization
Aortic insufficiency	Left ventricular enlargement	Left ventricular hypertrophy Tall R waves Sinus tachycardia	Left ventricular enlargement Abnormal mitral valve movement Increased movement of ventricular wall	Aortic regurgitation Increased LVEDP Decreased arterial diastolic pressure
Tricuspid stenosis	Right atrial enlargement Prominence of superior vena cava	Right atrial hypertrophy Tall peaked P waves Atrial fibrillation	Abnormal valvular leaflets Right atrial enlargement	Increased pressure gradient across valve Increased right atrial pressure Decreased CO
Tricuspid insufficiency	Right atrial enlargement Right ventricular enlargement	Right ventricular hypertrophy Atrial fibrillation	Prolapse of tricuspid valve Right atrial enlargement	Increased atrial pressure Tricuspid regurgitation Decreased CO

Reprinted with permission from *Medical Surgical Nursing* 3rd Ed, by Long, B et al. Copyright 1993 by C.V. Mosby Co. St. Louis.

Overview of Hemodynamic Presentation in Various Disease Entities

Disease/ Disorder	RR	HR	BP	PP	CO	CVP	PAP	PAWP	SVR	PVR	SvO₂
Adult respiratory distress syndrome	↑	↑	↓↑	↓↑	N	N	↑	N	N	↑	↓
Cardiac failure:											
LHF	↑	↑	↓↑	↓	↓	N/↑	↑	↑	↑	↑	↓
RHF	↑	↑	↓↑	↓	↓	↑	N	N	↑	N	↓
Cardiac tamponade	↑	↑	N/↓	↓	N/↓	↑	↑	↑	↑	N/↑	N/↓
Cardiomyopathy	↑	↑	N/↑	↓	N/↓	↑	↑	↑	↑	N/↑	N/↓
COPD	↑	↑	N	N	N/↓	N/↑	↑	N	N/↓	↑	↓
Myocardial infarction	N/↑	↑	↓↑	↓	N/↓	N/↑	N/↑	N/↑	↑	N/↑	N/↓
Pulmonary edema	↑	↑	↑	N/↓	N	N	↑	↑	↓↑	↑	↓
Pulmonary embolism	↑	↑	N	N	N	↑	↑	N	N	↑	N/↓
Shock:											
Anaphylactic	↑	↑	↓	↓	↓	↓	↓	↓	↓	N/↑	↓
Cardiogenic	↑	↑	↓	↓	↓	N	↓↑	↓↑	N/↑	N/↑	↓
Hypovolemic compensated	↑	↑	N/↑	N/↓	↓↑	↓↑	↓↑	↓↑	↑	↓	↓
Decompensated	↑	↑	↓	↓	↓	↓	↓	↓	↑	N/↑	↓
Neurogenic	↓↑	↓	↓	↓	N/↓	↓	↓	↓	↓	N/↑	↓
Septic (Warm)	↑	↑	N/↓	↑	N/↑	↓	↓↑	↓↑	↓	N/↑	↑
(Cold)	↑	↑	↓	↑	↓	↓	↓↑	↓↑	↓↑	N/↑	↓↑
Valular:											
Aortic stenosis	↑	↑	↓	↓	↓	N/↑	↑	↑	↑	↑	↓
Aortic regurgitation	↑	↑	↓	↓	↓	N/↑	↑	↑	N/↑	↑	↓
Mitral stenosis	N/↑	N/↑	N/↓	↓	N/↓	N/↑	N/↑	N/↑	N/↑	N/↑	N/↓
Mitral regurgitation	↑	N/↑	N/↑	↓	↓	N/↑	↑	↑	N/↑	N/↑	↓

Note: Considerable variation may exist

N = normal, ↑ = increased, ↓ = decreased, ↓↑ = variable

Diseases

Bibliography

ALBERT, R. K. ET.AL	*Comprehensive Respiratory Medicine, 1999*	C.V. Mosby Co.
HIGGINS, T. ET.AL.	*Cardiopulmonary Critical Care , 2002*	Bios Scientific Publishers.Ltd
DAILY, E. AND SCHROEDER, J.	*Techniques in Bedside Hemodynamic Monitoring, 5th Ed., 1994*	C.V. Mosby Co.
Darovic, G.	*Handbook of Hemodynamic Monitoring, 2nd Ed. 2004*	Saunders
DAROVIC, G.	*Hemodynamic Monitoring: Invasive and Noninvasive Clinical Application, 3rd Edition, 2002*	Saunders
GOLDMAN, L. ET. AL.	*Cecil Textbook of Medicine, 23rd Ed, 2007*	Saunders
HESS, D. & KACMAREK, R.	*Respiratory Care: Principles and Practices, 1st Ed., 2001*	Saunders
OAKES, D. F.	*Clinical Practitioners Pocket Guide to Respiratory Care, 7th Ed. 2008*	Health Educator Publications, Inc
QUELLET, P.	*Hemodynamics and Gas Exchange, 1991*	Marevie
RAKEL, R.E. & BOPE, E.T.	*Conn's Current Therapy, 2009*	Saunders
TIERNEY, L.M. ET. AL.	*Current Medical Diagnosis and Treatment 2006, 45th Ed., 2005*	McGraw-Hill Medical
TOPOL, E. ET. AL.	*Textbook of Cardiovascular Medicine, 3rd Ed. 2006*	Lippincott Williams & Wilkins
WILKINS, R. L. & STOLLER, J.K.	*Egan's Fundamentals of Respiratory Care, 9th Ed., 2008*	Mosby/Elsevier

Index

A-3